STRESS IN TEACHING

A Comparison of Perceived Occupational Stress Factors Between Special Education and Regular Classroom Teachers

Raymond V. D'Arienzo
Auburn City Schools

John C. Moracco
Auburn University

Robert J. Krajewski
University of Northern Iowa

UNIVERSITY
PRESS OF
AMERICA

Copyright © 1982 by
University Press of America, Inc.™
P.O. Box 19101, Washington, D.C. 20036

All rights reserved

Printed in the United States of America

ISBN (Perfect): 0-8191-1875-3
ISBN (Cloth): 0-8191-1874-5

Library of Congress Number 81-43711

Dedication

This text is dedicated to the thousands of teachers who face the daily stress of their profession. This challenge is met by most. It is a tribute on their dedication, courage, and faith.

Acknowledgements

The authors are grateful to the following Auburn University graduate students for their assistance: Deborah D. Danford, Gayle T. Gam, Alice Averette Hall, Guy Richardson, and Richard Lawrence Moore.

Appreciation is also extended to Professors Michael S. Littleford and Ray C. Phillips for their contributions, and guidance.

A note of thanks is offered to Brenda Gutgsell for her many hours of unselfish aid in the collection of data during the field study.

TABLE OF CONTENTS

PREFACE

I. INTRODUCTION

    Statement of the Problem 1
    Purpose of the Study 4
    Rational of the Study 5
    Definitions of Terms 6
    Hypotheses 7
    Limitations of the Study 8
    Organization of the Study 9

II. REVIEW OF LITERATURE

    Definitions of Stress 11
    Models of the Stress Process . . . 15
    Causes, Symptoms, and Effects . . . 16
        causes 16
        symptoms 26
        effects 28
    Coping Mechanisms 33
    Special Education Teachers and
        Stress 37
    Instruments Used in Stress Studies. 39
    Summary of the Review of
        Literature 44

III. METHODS

    Introduction 47
    Method 47
        Setting 47
        Sample 48
        Instrumentation 56
        Procedures 59
        Design of the Study 61
        Analysis of the Data 62

IV. RESULTS

    Teacher Absenteeism and Stress . . 63
    Comparison of Factor Analysis 64
      Procedures . . . .
    Regression Analyses of Predictor 75
      Variables . . . .
    Factor 1 77
    Factor 2 80
    Factor 3 82
    Factor 4 84
    Factor 5 85
    Summary of Results 88

V. DISCUSSION

    Factor Structure 93
    Predictor Variables 99
    Implication for Future Research . . 103

REFERENCES 107

APPENDICES

    A. Clark's (1980) TOSFQ 121

    B. Modified TOSFQ 126

    C. Table 24: Items TOSFQ and
        Their Factor Locations on
        TOSFQ and Modified TOSFQ . . 133

LIST OF FIGURES

    A Model of Stress 15

    Means and Standard Deviations of
      Modified TOSFQ Five Factors 76

LIST OF TABLES

1. Internal Consistency Coefficients for Each of the Five Factors 44
2. Surveyed Schools by Series Identification Number of Teachers Surveyed, Number of Respondents, and Respondent Percentage for Each School 50
3. Age of Sampled Teachers 54
4. Racial Composition of Sampled Teachers   55
5. Years of Teaching Experience of Sampled Teachers 56
6. Type of School 57
7. School Enrollment 58
8. Number of School Days Missed Reported by Respondents 64
9. Estimate of Percentage of Work Days Missed Due to Stress by 346 Respondents 65
10. Oblique Rotation Comparisons of Clark's TOSFQ and Present TOSFQ's First 30 Items 67
11. Factor Structure of Clark's TOSFQ and the Present TOSFQ 68
12. Factor Correlation Comparisons of TOSFQ and Modified TOSFQ 75
13. Summary of Multiple Regression Analysis Factor 1: Administrative Support 79

14.	Summary of Multiple Regression Analysis Factor 2: Working Students	81
15.	Means and Numbers for Types of Schools on Factor 2: Working With Students	82
16.	Summary of Multiple Regression Analysis Factor 3: Financial Security	83
17.	Summary of Multiple Regression Analysis Factor 4: Relationships With Teachers	86
18.	Summary of Multiple Regression Analysis Factor 5: Task Overload	87
19.	Means and Numbers for Types of Schools on Factor 5: Task Overload	88
20.	Significance Levels of the Eight Independent Variables Across the Five Factors of the Modified TOSFQ	90
21.	Decision to Reject the Eight Hypotheses Across the Five Factors of the Modified TOSFQ	92
22.	A Comparison of Stress Factors Among Three Studies	94
23.	Given values and Percentage of Variance of Present Study's Five Factors	98
24.	Items 1-30 and Their Factor Locations on TOSFQ and Modified TOSFQ	135

Preface

Emotional and physical tension are commonplace in America. All persons, regardless of the paths they travel, are subject to stress from time to time. Every occupation has its problems which provide a source for tension among its practitioners. Some occupations are more stress-filled than others. To an outsider, teaching might be considered one of those occupations in which the rigors of the job are among the less stressful. After all, what problems can be produced by working with groups of youngsters whose bright, shining faces and dancing eyes indicate their eagerness to learn? Who among us would not find continuous joy in satisfying a child's thirst for knowledge?

Unfortunately, the picture of teaching as a perennial source of pleasure is distorted. Teachers know that while there are great joys in teaching, the job also has its full share of physical, mental, and emotional pressures. This always has been true, despite the aura of Mr. Chips and Miss Peach. In recent years, the stress placed on teachers, both external and internal, has increased. The literature has begun to reflect this phenomenon as researchers have directed their attention to "teacher stress" and "teacher burnout."

In this volume the authors discuss factors which may be the sources of tension among teachers. Their research has taken us several steps forward, not only in the identification of sources of pressure, but also in providing teachers and administrators with a base for determining how to approach the problem of reducing the incidence of teacher burnout. While the research has significant value as a starting point for future exploration, it makes an equally significant contribution to the field of educational administration in that a careful reading can point the way for school administrators who daily must deal with teachers working under increasingly stressful conditions.

--John C. Walden
Auburn University
February, 1982

CHAPTER ONE

INTRODUCTION

Stress has been characterized as pleasant (eustress) or unpleasant (distress) (Selye, 1976). Unpleasant stress and its effects on educators were the main focus of this study. Concern for teacher stress is not a very recent phenomenon. Research studies on teacher stress, anxiety, and mental health first appeared in this country as early as 1933. Hicks' (1933) survey of 600 classroom teachers revealed that 17% of the respondents were "unusually nervous," and that an additional 11% had suffered nervous breakdowns. Peck's (1933) study revealed that 33% of the 110 female teachers surveyed suffered from nervous symptoms. The results of more recent studies indicate a substantial increase in the number of teachers who are experiencing stress. A 1967 study by the National Education Association (N.E.A.) reported that 78% of the teachers in the study experienced moderate or considerable levels of stress (Coates & Thoresen, 1976, p. 161). In an address to the 1977 annual convention of the American Association of School Administrators, teaching was included in the top three most potentially stressful occupations (Hunter, 1977). A 1978 Chicago teachers' union survey revealed that 56.6% of the 5,500 responding teachers stated they suffered from job related physical and/or mental illness (Walsh, 1979). Thus, stress is a formidable problem among today's teachers.

Statement of the Problem

Recent studies have indicated that teachers are leaving the profession at an alarming rate. The N.E.A. has estimated that 30% of the nation's teachers would prefer to be doing something other than teaching (Bardo, 1979), and that 40% of today's teachers say they will leave teaching before retirement (Muse, 1980). A more recent N.E.A. study revealed an increase in the aforementioned figures. This survey of 2,165 public school teachers representing all geographical parts of the country and all educational levels reported the following: (a) Only 43% of today's teachers plan to continue teaching until they are eligible for retirement; (b) From the 1,738 teachers responding, 9% stated that they are planning to leave the classroom as soon as possible; and (c) A full 41% said they would not choose the teaching profession if they had the choice to make again (N.E.A., 1980).

Not only has the amount of stress experienced by teachers increased, but also the intensity. "The intensity of this stress [job related] has never been higher; its potential for undermining the instructional process in the public schools has never been more ominous" (Ban, 1980, p. 1). The problem of teacher stress has become so serious that in Tacoma, Washington, a local teachers' association has been successful in negotiating stress insurance for its members (Tacoma's Stress, 1979). N.E.A. has recognized teacher stress as a societal concern, and in 1980 its Representative Assembly adopted Resolution E-42 which recognized the increase in the emotional and physical disabilities caused by stress among school teachers. Furthermore, the N.E.A. resolution urged the local authorities and teacher associations to develop stress management programs to help teachers cope with stress (Muse, 1980).

Today the problem of teacher stress is being addressed in a more honest and open fashion than it has been in the past. The taboos associated with stress and the myth of teacher tranquility are finally being laid to rest. "The studies on teacher burnout proliferate and now constitute a sizeable portion of the total research into occupational stress. Additionally, teacher organizations have speeded their search to assist teachers in handling the problem" (Ban, 1980, p. 2).

Concern over teacher stress has not been limited to local and national teacher groups. On February 6, 1980, the United States House of Representatives Sub-Committee on Elementary, Secondary, and Vocational Education heard testimony regarding occupational stress among teachers. The testimony, presented by Marsha Berger, Vice President At Large, Providence Teachers' Union, included a plea for additional research on conditions producing teacher stress, and pointed out the need to provide professional help to teachers who have experienced severe stress (Berger, 1980).

Despite the tremendous amount of research and energy which has been devoted to the understanding of teacher stress, the research is still in its infancy, and there is a need for developing a clear definition and model of teacher stress before research can be carried out meaningfully (Kyriacou & Sutcliffe, 1978, p. 1). Others agree. Burchfield (1979) recommends that a stress research moratorium be enacted until a more precise definition and theory of stress can be agreed upon. Total agreement may never be reached, and to postpone or delay investigative educational research concerning a phenomenon which affects such a large number of classroom teachers may not be prudent. Although consensus has not been reached, definitions of teacher stress have been offered by a number of educational researchers.

The emotional and/or psychosomatic, as well as physical, conditions resulting from stress are well documented (Bloch, 1978; Muse, 1979, 1980; Newell, 1979; Selye, 1976; Walsh, 1979). The effects of prolonged psychic stress of teachers have been likened to the effects experienced by survivors of war disasters suffering from combat neurosis. Physiologically, stress causes problems in the body's cardiovascular, digestive, immunological, and skeletal-muscular systems (Muse, 1980). Doctors have also associated stress with general anxiety, tension, depression, addiction to alcohol and other drugs, breakdowns in collegial and family relationships, friendships, low job productivity, absenteeism from the job, hospitalization, and ultimately premature death (Newell, 1979). Additionally, most teacher absenteeism is due to stress related mental health problems (Harlin & Jerrick, 1976).

Stress, as perceived by special education teachers, was of specific importance to this study. The literature reveals many studies of stress experienced by classroom teachers, school administrators, and counselors. However, a perusal of the literature has indicated that until very recently virtually nothing has been written concerning stress and the special education teacher. Recent federal and state regulations have provided a new emphasis on special education and have generated the initiation of various special education programs across the country. The lack of research and the newly provided emphasis on special education were the cornerstones upon which the rationale for and purposes of this study were based.

Purpose of the Study

The primary purpose of the study was to investigate the differences between special education and other classroom teachers' perceptions of occupational stress factors.

Secondary purposes of the study were to ascertain what differences exist between teachers' belief systems about themselves and their students, and certain demographic variables. Besides Teacher Belief Systems, the variables include Marital Status, Years Teaching Experience, Sex of Principal, Obsessive-Compulsive Ideations, School Setting, and Type of School.

More specifically, this study collected data to answer the following research questions:

1. Do special education teachers perceive stress differently from other classroom teachers?

2. Do the stated demographic variables affect teacher's perceptions of stress?

Teachers' scores on the "Teacher Occupational Stress Factor Questionnaire" (TOSFQ) and the four additional sections (teachers' feelings, symptoms, coping mechanisms, and demographics) were analyzed in both descriptive and inferential fashion. Demographic data were analyzed to ascertain the differences on each of the variables for the sample.

Rationale for the Study

Since "the problems of stress and tension experienced by teachers are real, prevalent, and potentially deleterious to teachers and students" (Coates & Thoresen, 1976, p. 176), there was a need to more clearly define the occupational stress factors as perceived by teachers. Once these perceptions are identified, teachers should better understand the occupational stress factors affecting them. Clark has stated, "Once the occupational stress factors for teachers have been identified, efforts at helping teachers develop strategies to alleviate, minimize, and cope can commence" (1980, p. 7).

Important to the present study was also the fact that teachers are leaving the profession and/or want to leave because they may be victims of professional burnout caused by the multitude of stressors they must cope with each day (Walsh, 1979). Subsequently, education is experiencing a shortage of veteran teachers. In a period of less than 15 years (1962-1976) the percentage of teachers with 20 or more years of experience has been reduced 50% (Walsh, 1979). Also significant is the fact that 30% of all teachers, if given the opportunity, would prefer to be doing something else (Bardo, 1979). "Locating the source of stress has in itself a therapeutic effect" (Clark, 1980, p. 7). This therapeutic effect may enable effective teachers to remain and want to remain in the profession longer.

Education, like every other profession, needs the benefits provided by experience. It cannot continue to suffer the loss of experienced teachers at the current rate as discussed by Walsh (1979). She suggests teachers are leaving because of professional burnout. This assumption, well documented in the literature, has provided educational research with the responsibility of determining the perceptions teachers have concerning stress, if for no other reason than, "The mere fact of knowing what hurts has a curative value" (Selye, 1976, p. 89). "The importance of mentally healthy teachers cannot be overstated" (Bentz, Hollister, & Edgerton, 1971, p. 72).

Definitions of Terms

For the purpose of this research, the following terms have been defined:

1. Elementary teacher--A professional person certified and employed to instruct in grades K-6.

2. Homeostasis--"The maintenance of the body's physiological resting state" (Burchfield, 1979, p. 661).

3. Obsessive-Compulsive Ideation-Psychological characteristics of perfectionistic attitudes held by individuals (Burns, 1980).

4. Occupational stressor--Anything which causes or is perceived to cause stress in the work environment.

5. Principal--A professional person certified and employed to be a school level chief administrator.

6. Secondary teacher--A professional person certified and employed to instruct in grades 7-12.

7. Special education--Services and programs provided to eligible students identified as handicapped as a result of emotional, physical, and/or intellectual impairments.

8. Special education teacher--A professional person certified and employed to instruct special education students.

9. Stress--An alteration of psychological homeostasis which is usually accompanied by physiological changes; these changes result from aspects of the teacher's job and are mediated by the perception that the demands upon the teacher are threats to well-being or self-esteem, and by psychological coping mechanisms employed to maintain homeostasis (Moracco & McFadden, 1980, p. 5).

10. Stress factor--"Variables or questionnaire items which cluster around an underlying theme when factor analyzed" (Clark, 1980, p. 12).

11. Teacher--A professional person certified to teach in grades K-12.

12. Teacher-Belief System--Personality characteristics considered peculiar to teachers. The Belief System Scale (items 31-40 on Modified TOSFQ used in this study) was designed to measure compulsive behavior specific to teaching.

Hypotheses

In order to ascertain and compare the perceptions of teachers concerning occupational stress factors, the following hypotheses were tested in this study:

Hypothesis1: There is no significant difference in mean scores between special education and other classroom teachers on each of the occupational stress factors.

Hypothesis 2: There is no significant difference between mean scores of teachers who teach in rural, urban, or suburban school settings with respect to each of the occupational stress factors.

Hypothesis 3: There is no significant difference between mean scores of teachers who teach in elementary, middle/junior high, high, senior high schools, and special education schools (centers) with respect to each of the occupational stress factors.

Hypothesis 4: There is no significant difference between mean scores of teachers who teach in schools having male principals and teachers who teach in schools having female principals with respect to each of the occupational stress factors.

Hypothesis 5: There is no significant difference between mean scores of single, married, divorced, or widowed teachers with respect to each of the occupational stress factors.

Hypothesis 6: There is no significant difference between mean scores of teachers who have 1-5, 6-10, 11-15, 16-20, or more than 21 years teaching experience with respect to each occupational stress factor.

Hypothesis 7: There is no significant relationship between mean scores of teachers' belief systems and each occupational stress factor.

Hypothesis 8: There is no significant relationship between mean scores of teachers' obsessive-compulsive ideations and each occupational stress factor.

Limitations of the Study

This study was limited in the following respects:

1. It was assumed that all teachers who completed the questionnaire did so in a sincere and honest manner. This study's accuracy was limited to the degree which respondents expressed true feelings when responding.

2. The study did not investigate teachers' perceptions of occupational stress factors, Obsessive-Compulsive Ideation, Teacher Belief Systems, etc., and their relationship to teachers' past experiences, intelligence, personality type, morale, etc.

3. The sample response was not 100%. Of the 1,335 teachers who participated in the study, 691 returned completed usable surveys for a response rate of 51.76%.

4. The generalization of the findings may be limited because the study's geographical area was confined to one administrative area of a large suburban school district located near Washington, D.C.

5. The study was limited to only those teachers who voluntarily participated.

6. Two principals from the 24 randomly selected elementary schools refused permission to conduct the study in their schools. Two additional elementary schools had to be randomly selected. One of the three participating senior high schools did not return any survey responses after agreeing to participate in the study.

Organization of the Study

The research has been organized into five chapters. Chapter 1, Introduction, consists of a statement of the problem, nature and purpose of the study, rationale for the study, definitions of terms, hypotheses, limitations of the study, and organization of the study.

Chapter II, Review of the Literature, considers both published and unpublished works on occupational stress with a special emphasis on relevant research in the area of teacher stress. In this chapter are included definitions of stress and burnout; causes, symptoms, and effects of stress; stress controllers and coping mechanisms; models of stress; and various instruments used in stress research. Special attention is given to the literature concerning the construction, scaling, and validation of the TOSFQ, the basis of the instrument used in this study. Chapter III, Methods, explains the study's setting, sample, instrument, and design. Additionally, the research and the statistical procedures employed are explained.

Chapter IV, Results, includes a presentation of the findings of this study and the statistical analyses of the data.

Chapter V, Discussion, summarizes the findings of this study, the conclusions that can be drawn from those findings, and discusses the implications for future research.

II. REVIEW OF THE LITERATURE

The purpose of this chapter is to investigate the literature on teacher occupational stress. This review examines models of the stress process, definitions, causes, symptoms and effects of stress and burnout. Coping mechanisms (both positive and negative) and stress as related to special education teachers are presented. Finally, instruments used in stress studies are presented.

Definitions of Stress

Stress is not unique to teachers or to the teaching profession. Everyone experiences stress to some degree. There are numerous definitions of stress. Broder (1979) says it is a "given" of life. Selye defines stress as "the nonspecific response of the body to any demand" (1976, p. 472). Lenci, of General Electric's Corporate Medical Operation, concurs, but adds: "Stress is the state you are in, not the agent which produces it" (Good vs. Bad, 1978, p. 38). Burchfield posits stress "as anything which causes an alteration of psychological homeostatic processes" (1979, p. 662).

Kyriacou and Sutcliffe define teacher stress as "a response of a negative affect (such as anger or depression) by a teacher usually accom-panied by potentially pathogenic physiological and biochemical changes . . . resulting from aspects of the teacher's job and mediated by the perception that the demands made upon the teacher constitute a threat to his self-esteem or well-being and by coping mechanisms activated to reduce the perceived threat" (1978, p. 2). Synthesizing, Moracco and McFadden have defined teacher stress as:

an alteration of psychological homeostasis usually accompanied by physiological changes resulting from aspects of the teacher's job and mediated by the perception that the demands upon the teacher are threats to self-esteem or well-being, and by psychological coping mechanisms employed to maintain homeostasis (1980, p. 5).

Newell describes stress as "an adaptation of the body to cope with psychic demands (fears, frustration, pain, grief, job pressures, marital discord) or somatic demands (surgical operations, burns, loss of blood). Job related stress is primarily the result of psychic demands" (1979, p. 16). A more recent definition offered by Alley states:

> Stress is a condition of everyone's life. . . . Stress is an integral part of living. It is the driving force which enables people to successfully meet the challenges of day to day duties. Indeed, those who do not experience stress are, by definition, dead. . . . Life is a series of unknowable and often unexpected events, both good and bad. As these events occur, human organisms must react to them. This reaction and particularly the bodily response to the unexpected or unknown is defined as stress (1980, p. 3).

As noted, stress can be conceptualized as pressure from outside that can make one feel tense inside. Stress is unavoidable and some of it is good. Ban's definition, "stress is the response of the body to demands placed upon it" (1980, p. 3), is as succinct as any discovered in the literature search, but for purposes of this study, Moracco and McFadden's more comprehensive definition of stress will be utilized.

Models of the Stress Process

Different models of teacher stress are discussed in the literature. The engineering model (Cox, 1978; Hinkle, 1974; Wield & Hanes, 1976) views stress in terms of the impact of the environment on an individual (Kyriacou & Sutcliffe, 1978). Clark reports that the physiological model appears to be "more widely accepted among social scientists than the engineering model" (1980, p. 17). Others (Kyriacou & Sutcliffe, 1978; Moracco & McFadden, 1980) suggest that most models of stress are quite similar, "and in many cases one can be substituted for another by simply changing the nomenclature" (Moracco & McFadden, 1980, pp. 5-6).

For purposes of this study, the Moracco and McFadden (1980) Model of Stress is discussed in detail because it is a comprehensive approach to the study at hand, i.e., teacher stress. The model is an adaptation of Kyriacou and Sutcliffe's (1978) model. It differs from the Kyriacou and Sutcliffe model in that it incorporates the cognitive aspects of the Burchfield (1979) model.

A Model of Stress (Moracco & McFadden, 1980) is represented in Figure 1. According to the model, Circle 1, "Potential Stressors," and its three components--"Societal," "Occupational," and "Home"--represent the three major arenas from which sources of stress emanate. Box 2, "Appraisal Mechanism," illustrates the process that a teacher uses to determine which potential stressors become actual stressors. If the potential source of stress is viewed as a threat to the teacher's well-being or self-esteem, it then becomes an actual stressor (Box 3). It is important to note that potential stressors affect teachers differently. The appraisal mechanisms of each teacher are mediated by several different forces (sex, age, past experiences). These will be discussed in greater detail when Box 7, "Individual Characteristics," is described. Box 3, "Actual Stressors," represents those potential stressors, real or not, which have been perceived by the teacher as a threat to his/her self-esteem or well-being. Thus they become actual stressors. "The appraisal process is influenced largely by whether or not the teacher feels he/she can meet the demands of the job or that the demands conflict with higher order needs" (Moracco & McFadden, 1980, p. 6). Once a stressor is perceived to be a threat, the person's coping mechanisms (Box 4) become important in how successful the teacher will be in reducing stress. "How well the stressful event is reduced has implications for manifestations of teacher's stress located in Box 5, 'Manifestations of Stress'" (Moracco & McFadden, 1980, p. 7). If the teacher employs ineffective coping mechanisms, the behavioral, physical, and/or psychological manifestations of stress will be prolonged and more severe. According to the model, prolonged manifestations will eventually lead to burnout and its chronic symptoms (Box 6).

As mentioned previously, "Individual Characteristics," will greatly determine how successfully the stressed teacher will cope. These characteristics, past experiences, personality traits, and belief systems, also will determine how severely the manifestations of stress will affect the the teacher who is experiencing it. If these characteristics do not provide adequate coping mechanisms, the individual probably will experience the more severe effects of the stress-burnout process discussed previously in this chapter. Figure 1 illustrates the Moracco and McFadden (1980) Model of Stress.

Stress and burnout, though related, are not equivalent terms. When stress becomes severe, fatigue or burnout sets in and a person undergoes a loss of energy, some flexibility, and even resourcefulness. Burnout, then, is "an overall feeling of helplessness, of losing self-control, of being overwhelmed and made helpless" (Ban, 1980, p. 3). It is basically the ultimate effect of continued stress. And, relatedly, the definition has been extended to helping professionals, in which job burnout is seen as "the emotional

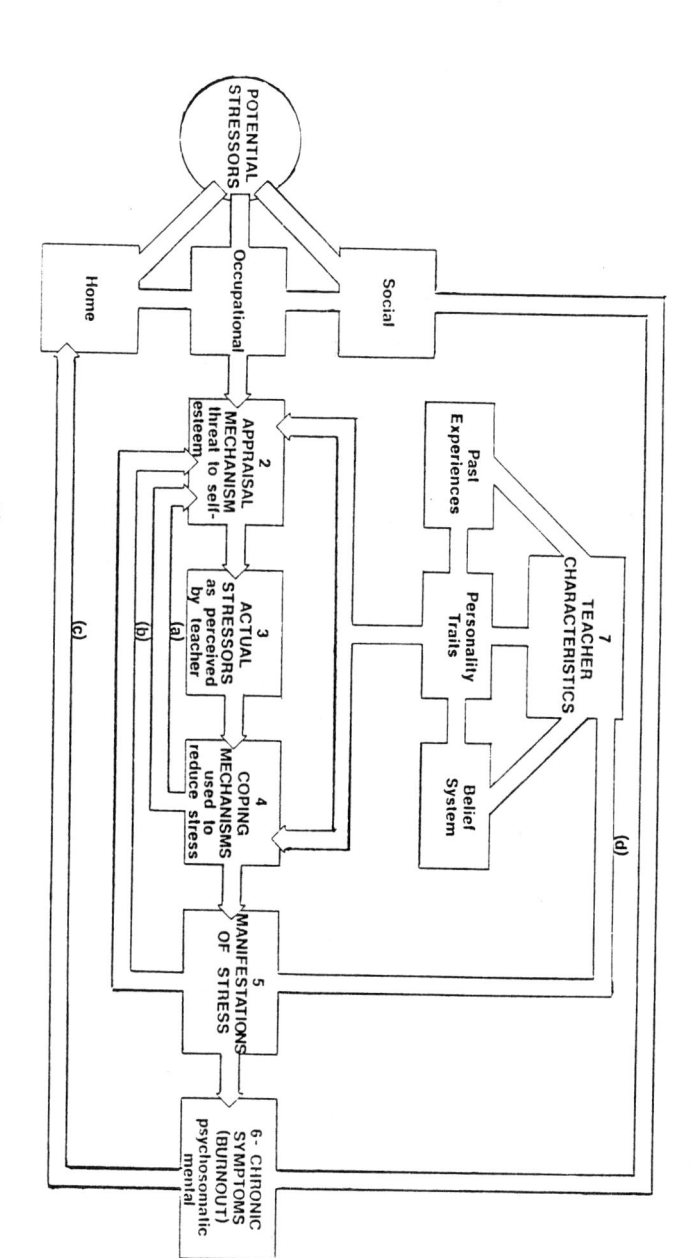

Figure 1 A Model of Teacher Stress

exhaustion resulting from the stress of interpersonal contact" (Maslach, 1978, p. 56). Time Magazine concurs: "It [burnout] is a psychological condition produced by stress" (Help! Teacher, 1980, p. 59). Anderson's definition of burnout, "physical and mental exhaustion resulting from on-the-job stress" (1980, p. 20) reinforces those previously listed.

Within the rubric of burnout is the more specific term, "teacher burnout," a condition caused by anxiety, stress, and tension. These problems are everyday encounters for teachers; unfortunately, teachers receive little or no help in coping with them (McGuire, 1979). The literature is replete with documentation asserting that teachers who experience continued stress eventually burn out. Collins has reported the following:

> Although there are many definitions and explanations for burnout, the most succinct explanation is that burnout is a complete physical, emotional and/or attitudinal exhaustion caused by excessive demands upon one's energy, emotions and resources (1981, p. 2).

Causes, Symptoms, and Effects

Causes

It would be naive to assume that teachers suffer from only job related or occupational stress. (See Figure 1, Circle 2.) Similar to people in all walks of life, teachers experience both on and off the job stress. Stress is a necessary and natural life ingredient.

Causes of potential stress, other than occupational, can be found in the model as home and/or societal environments. A major source of stress is change (McLean, 1973; Sylwester, 1977). Life's changes can initiate either pleasant or unpleasant stress within people. Sources (causes) of unpleasant stress, commonly referred to as distress, are of importance to this study. The concept of pleasant stress (eustress) is not discussed; the term "stress" is used to mean unpleasant stress.

"The Life Events Inventory," an often utilized predictor of stress-related dysfunction, lists 55 life events associated with varying amounts of disruption in the average person's life (Cochrane & Robertson, 1973). Such life changes as being sentenced to jail, experiencing the death of a spouse or other family member, to having a quarrel with neighbors, or going away for the holidays are included. Selye (1974) suggests that any event in one's life which causes a change or requires some readjustment is stress producing.

Teachers are not immune to societal and home potential stressors. Like others, they experience family problems, own automobiles which fail to start on a cold morning or break down on a lonely highway late at night, have financial concerns, receive speeding tickets, wait in gas lines, become victims of crime and assault in the streets, and pay income and property taxes. Teachers, therefore, experience no more or less societal and home environmental stressors than do non-teachers. It must be assumed that an interrelationship exists among the various causes of stress, but the difference is in the amount of occupational stress teachers experience. Therefore, a main concern of this study is to investigate the occupational sources of stress in the teaching profession.

Cichon and Koff (1978) identify four clusters of stressors in the teaching profession. These clusters include the following: "priority concerns," "management tension concerns," "doing-a-good-job concerns," and "pedagogical functions concerns."

Within the priority concerns cluster, Cichon and Koff include disruptive students, threats of personal injury, student assaults on teachers, and verbal abuse by students. The dominant themes are violence and student discipline.

The second cluster, management tension, includes involuntary transfers, disagreements with supervisors, denial of promotion or advancement, overcrowded classrooms, lack of books and supplies, notice of unsatisfactory performance, reorganization of programs and classes, and implementation of local boards of education goals and policies. This cluster represents actions, events, and situations which teachers have little or no control over. Realistically, "these events represent stress which is 'imposed' upon the teacher in the form of action constraints" (Cichon & Koff, 1978, p. 9). The results of their study, in which the degree of stress induced by each event was rank-ordered, showed involuntary transfers to be the number one inducer of stress for teachers.

The doing-a-good-job cluster of events includes teaching below average children and maintaining self-control when angry. Both are considered to be important professional responsibilities of teachers.

The fourth area of concern, the pedagogical functions cluster, is usually perceived by teachers to be the least stressful. This cluster, the 10 lowest ranked events in the study, includes teacher-parent conferences, lesson plans, problems concerning bilingual students, additional coursework for promotion, discussion of students' problems with their parents, conferences with the principal, student evaluations, and in-service meetings.

From their research, Cichon and Koff state:

> One might infer from these data that teachers find less stressful those teaching events (i.e., pedagogical functions) over which they have direct control. Conversely, stress induced by central administrative mandates (and

inefficiencies) and by state and federal regulations, over which teachers have little control, interferes with their optimal performance in the most critical aspects of their roles (1978, p. 11).

The writings and research of others offer credence to the Cichon and Koff study. Studies of job related--environmental, interpersonal, and intrapersonal--sources of stress for teachers proliferate the literature. Acts of crime, such as assaults on teachers by students, threats of bodily injury, violent acts, and vandalism are perceived by teachers to to be stressful (Ban, 1980; Bloch, 1978; Goodall & Brown, 1980; McGuire, 1979; N.E.A., 1980; Stevenson & Milt, 1975; Teacher burnout, 1979).

> Some students attack the school in ways that amount to guerrilla warfare. Attacks on personal property (thefts, malicious mischief, and arson) cost as much as $590 million annually, including increased insurance costs, security guards, sophisticated electronic surveillance equipment, and the expense of repairs and replacements. That is equivalent to a vandalism tax of $13 levied for every public school student. The human toll from the guerrilla warfare is equally staggering. Each year over 52,000 (5 percent) of the nation's one million secondary teachers are attacked, 10,000 of whom require medical treatment; 60,000 teachers (6 percent) are robbed; and every month 120,000 have something stolen (cited in Alschuler, 1980, p. 8).

Such acts of violence committed by students and others in the schools indeed are a major source of stress for teachers, and there are many other sources. Maintaining classroom discipline and dealing with disruptive students are further examples of interpersonal sources of stress (Alley, 1980; Anderson, 1980; Ban, 1980; Bloch,

1978; Broder, 1979; Coates & Thoresen, 1976; Goodall & Brown, 1980; McGuire, 1979; Readers report, 1979; Sylwester, 1977; Wey, 1951).

Discipline and classroom control are a major source of interpersonal stress for teachers at all grade levels. In many instances, they are dealing with students from varied backgrounds, some of whom have had few personal contraints placed on them before their school experience. Although the public, parents, and administrators demand educational accountability, educators have to contend with many discipline problems which take time away from teaching. Some children, for example, have emotional difficulties, and some have developed a negative attitude toward learning and school. When pupil misbehavior interrupts and/or interferes with the teaching-learning process, pressure and tension result, thus adding to teacher stress (Swick & Hanley, 1980, p. 12).

Too much parental interference and too little cooperation from parents also are considered sources of stress for teachers (Bloch, 1977; McGuire, 1979; Teacher burnout, 1979). Disagreements and conflicts with peers, administrators, and supervisors are perceived as stressful by teachers (Alley, 1980; Anderson, 1980; Ban, 1980; Yuenger, 1981). Recent federal legislation, specifically the passage of Public Law 94-142, has presented classroom teachers with yet another source of interpersonal stress. Mainstreaming of handicapped and other special needs students is forcing regular classroom teachers to teach children and cope with particular problems for which they have not been adequately trained (Bensky, Shaw, Gouse, Bates, Dixon & Beane, 1980; Readers report, 1979; Sylwester, 1977; Weiskopf, 1980). "With limited training in special education and and influx of special students into their classes, regular teachers may be experiencing additional stress" (Weiskopf, 1980, p. 2).

Teaching is a people-oriented process. Teachers must interact with students, parents, colleagues, school administrators, and supervisors continually. "The cost to teachers of attempting to be all things to all people may be a heavy dose of guilt, frustration, and tension" (Sparks, 1979a, p. 448). There is very little time during the hectic school day when teachers have a chance to be alone to reflect or to just simply collect their thoughts. Continuous interactions with various groups require teachers to master many communication skills and assume a variety of oftentimes conflicting roles. "Teachers are perpetually expected to be diplomats, mediators, counselors, disciplinarians, and imparters of knowledge" (Swick & Hanley, 1980, p. 14). They also are expected to be policemen, surrogate parents, and older siblings. Assuming these roles is not easy and it may produce a great deal of stress for teachers. Kahn (1973) reports that jobs requiring extensive communication with diverse groups are potentially highly stressful. These sources of stress are mediated by the Teacher's Belief Systems (see Figure 1). If the teacher has Obsessive-Compulsive Ideations, it is then likely that the events will be appraised as stressful. This is an example of how belief systems can influence teachers' perceptions of stress.

Swick and Hanley (1980) state that teachers experience intrapersonal and environmental sources of stress in addition to interpersonal sources. Intrapersonal stressors are associated with self-concept, motivation, the teacher's education, and classroom skills. Hodge and Marker (cited in Swick & Hanley, 1980) describe intrapersonal stressors as sources of stress which basically arise from how teachers feel about themselves, i.e., feelings of personal adequacy. Experiencing too many intrapersonal stressors eventually may cause teachers to lose their self-confidence as professionals.

Intrapersonal stress emanating from experiencing overwhelming feelings of helplessness, powerlessness, worthlessness, and having no control over their professional situations may be the single most important source of stress for teachers (Alley, 1980; Ban, 1980; Bardo, 1980; Berger, 1980; Broder, 1979; Cardinell, 1980; Harrison, 1980; Kotsakis, 1978; Newell, 1979; Sparks, 1979a). Intrapersonal sources of stress also relate to the expectations and goals which teachers set for themselves. Within this realm of self-expectations, Styles and Cavanagh believe that stress is generated by:

> (i) the teacher's fear that he or she will not be able to live up to his or her own expectations, or up to the expectations of others.
> (ii) the habit of setting overly high or cynically low expectations.
> (iii) the feeling that the personal achievements and successes of yesterday are not good enough for today.
> (iv) the teachers' fears that they will be found wanting because they are insufficiently flexible and innovative in their instructional methods (1977, p. 76).

Feeling that they cannot successfully meet accountability and time demands is yet another source of intrapersonal stress for teachers (Ban, 1980; Coates & Thoresen, 1976; Cooper & Marshall, 1976; Leffingwell, 1979; Stevenson & Milt, 1975). With the sundry curricular demands placed upon them, teachers sometimes feel constrained in reaching desired expectations. The expectations others have of the teacher's role are not always congruent with those the teacher anticipates in his/her professional role. Thus another source of intrapersonal stress appears (Ban, 1980; Readers report, 1979). Role conflict or role ambiguity is a leading intrapersonal stressor affecting teachers (Cooper & Marshall, 1976; Miles, 1976). One study delineates:

> The effects of role conflict...are varied in form but consistently negative in their implications for the focal person. Persons subjected to high role conflict report greater job-related tensions, lower job satisfaction, less confidence in the organization itself, and more intense experience of conflict (Kahn, 1973, p. 5).

As stated earlier, intrapersonal stress arises from inadequate feelings about oneself. Whether such stressors are personal (off the job) or professsional (on the job), they are a serious inducer of stress (cited in Swick & Hanley, 1980). These feelings affect people differently. Below is how one teacher was affected by feelings of inadequacy:

> Bill, a junior high school math teacher, may notice on a particular morning that many of his students are shuffling their feet and look disinterestedly out the window . . . Some teachers might simply ignore this, or even fail to notice it. But to Bill these student behaviors represent apathy and boredom. He suddenly imagines (anticipates) being sharply criticized by the principal because he has heard the principal say many times, 'If you cannot hold the students' interest, then you have no business being a teacher' . . . Bill's principal has been known to call this to the attention of his teachers in public. Bill finds himself sweating, stuttering, and worrying about how inadequate he is as a teacher . . . The cycle accelerates and he becomes more and more tense and more irritated. Finally, he bruskly assigns some lengthy seatwork and retreats to his desk to correct papers (or perhaps shuffle them) (Hendricks, Thoresen, & Coates, 1975, pp. 4-5).

In summary, whether an event is viewed as stressful is largely determined or influenced by the individual characteristics of the teacher. This in turn is influenced by the teacher's particular belief and personality systems. (See Figure 1, A Model of Stress, for an explanation of this process.)

In addition to interpersonal and intrapersonal sources of stress, teachers also are affected by environmental stressors. Environmental stressors are those sources of stress and tension which are found within the school environment or organization (Stevenson & Milt, 1975; Swick & Hanley, 1980). They are a prominent source of stress to teachers because they are inherent within schools and are perceived by teachers as sources of stress over which they have little or no control. Environmental stressors are those ingredients within the teaching profession which, when mixed together, produce "a situation best characterized as 'responsibility without control'" (Collins, 1980, p. 2). The fear of being involuntarily transferred to another school is a leading environmental source of stress for teachers (Bloch, 1977; Cichon & Koff, 1978; McGuire, 1979; Survey analysis, 1978; Teacher burnout, 1979; Yuenger, 1981). Recent legislation and judicial decisions have forced many school systems across the nation to desegregate their student populations and their faculties. The involuntary teacher transfer is one means school systems have utilized to comply with these decisions. Thus, teachers who are transferred are victims of imposed stress.

Involuntary transfer of teachers is a procedure used by the Board [Chicago] for the purpose of trying to comply with desegregation guidelines. Teachers must, except through the process of appeal, accept the Board's directive to move to another school. When someone is directed to move from one work site to another, it goes without saying that the directive (or the likelihood of being told one will be transferred) carries with it a considerable amount of stress (Cichon & Koff, 1978, pp. 9-10).

Feeling that they work for inadequate salaries is another environmental stressor for teachers (Alley, 1980; Ban, 1980; Cichon & Koff, 1978; Coates & Thoresen, 1976; Collins, 1981; Goodall & Brown, 1980; McGuire, 1979; N.E.A., 1967; Stevenson & Milt, 1975). Perceiving that there is a lack of mobility in education and that their job is a dead-end situation provides teachers with even more environmental stress (Ban, 1980; Cooper & Marshall, 1976; Readers report, 1979; Yuenger, 1981). Closely associated with this perception is the fear teachers have of being the recipient of a poor evaluation, or of being denied the opportunity of promotion or advancement (Ban, 1980; Cichon & Koff, 1978; Survey analysis, 1978). The physical teaching environment itself, often consisting of inadequate or run down facilities which confine teachers to oversized classes in close quarters, produces its own environmental source of stress for teachers (Ban, 1980; Berger, 1980; Bloch, 1977; Cichon & Koff, 1978; Coates & Thoresen, 1976; Collins, 1981; Cooper & Marshall, 1976; McGuire, 1979; Survey analysis, 1978; Tacoma's stress, 1979; Yuenger, 1981). Lack of textbooks and inadequate instructional supplies produce stress in classroom teachers (Berger, 1980; Cichon & Koff, 1978; Newell, 1979; Olander & Farrell, 1970; Sparks, 1979a; Survey analysis, 1978). Excessive paperwork demands in teaching have become monumental, thus becoming an additional source of stress (Alley, 1980; Berger, 1980; Collins, 1981; Kotsakis, 1978; McGuire, 1979; Walsh, 1979; Weiskopf, 1980; Yuenger, 1981).

Classroom teachers state that lack of administrative support and/or poor leadership and organization are other environmental stressors (Anderson, 1980; Bloch, 1977; Broder, 1979; Cichon & Koff, 1978; Kotsakis, 1978; Newell, 1979; Readers report, 1979; Sparks, 1979a; Weiskopf, 1980). Being isolated from fellow workers (Ban, 1980) and becoming a victim of the educational bureaucracy with its almost continuous reorganization of programs (including mainstreaming) and classes (Collins, 1981; Readers report, 1979; Survey analysis, 1978; Sylwester, 1977; Weiskopf, 1980; Yuenger, 1981) also are environmental stressors. Considering the multitudes of stressors experienced by teachers, it is "No wonder fear, insecurity, and anxiety are replacing the joy of teaching" (McGuire, 1979, p. 5).

Symptoms

Symptoms of stress are sometimes subtle, sometimes obvious, sometimes mild, and sometimes severe, but in too many cases, "stress will frequently manifest itself in the syndrome now commonly referred to as burnout" (Collins, 1981, p. 2). Manifestations of the stress-burnout process are exhibited physically, psychologically, and/or behaviorally (Moracco & McFadden, 1980). (See Figure 1, Box 5.) Examples of physical manifestations include the following: respiratory illness, such as shortness of breath (Bloch, 1977, 1978; Cardinell, 1980; Dale, 1976); stomach problems, for example, peptic ulcers (Bloch, 1977, 1978; CTU survey, 1978; Dale, 1976); frequent headaches, including sinus and migraine varieties (Berger, 1980; Bloch, 1977; Broder, 1979; Harlin, 1976; Moracco & McFadden, 1980); cardiovascular diseases, including increased heart rate and hypertension (Berger, 1980; Bloch, 1977, 1978; Broder, 1979; Cooper & Marshall, 1976; CTU survey, 1978; Dale, 1976); and total fatigue, a mental and physical exhaustion which doesn't disappear even with a "good night's sleep" (Alley, 1980; Ban, 1980; Bartley, 1975; Berger, 1980; Bloch, 1977; Broder, 1979; Cardinell, 1980; Cherry, 1978; Dixon et al., 1980; Harlin, 1976; Hendrickson, 1979). Other physical manifestations are various skin irritations (Berger, 1980; Leffingwell, 1979); unusual loss or gain in body weight (Broder, 1979; Cardinell, 1980; Hendrickson, 1979); dizziness (Bloch, 1977); insomnia (Bardo, 1979; Cardinell, 1980; CTU survey, 1978; Leffingwell, 1979; Moracco

& McFadden, 1980; Seyle, 1978); and blurred vision (Bloch, 1977).

Psychological manifestations of the stress-burnout process are as follows: depression (Berger, 1980; Cardinell, 1980; Cooper & Marshall, 1976; Harlin, 1976; Hendrickson, 1979; Maslach, 1978; Moracco & McFadden, 1980; Weiskopf, 1980); anxiety and emotional tension, including a lowered tolerance for frustration (Berger, 1980; Bloch, 1977; Cardinell, 1980; Moracco & McFadden, 1980); low self-esteem, including general feelings of worthlessness, insecurity, and helplessness (Alley, 1980; Ban, 1980; Bardo, 1979; Berger, 1980; Cardinell, 1980; Freudenberger, 1977; Harrison, 1980; Leffingwell, 1979; Maslach, 1978; Moracco & McFadden, 1980); various phobias and general symptoms of paranoia (Bloch, 1977; Cardinell, 1980; Freudenberger, 1977; Moracco & McFadden, 1980); cognitive impairment, including confused thinking, denial of reality, and increased difficulty in making decisions rationally (Alley, 1980; Bloch, 1977; Leffingwell, 1979; Moracco & McFadden, 1980); and nightmares and startled responses (Bloch, 1977, 1978). Experiencing marital and family problems (Freudenberger, 1977; Leffingwell, 1979; Maslach, 1978; Weiskopf, 1980); loss of sexual interest (Hendrickson, 1979); boredom (Freudenberger, 1977; Weiskopf, 1980); feelings of being overworked and overwhelmed (Leffingwell, 1979; Weiskopf, 1980); and sometimes even total emotional breakdown (Hendrickson, 1979) are additional psychological manifestations which frequent the literature. Moodiness (Cardinell, 1980; Harlin, 1976) and increased irritability (Bloch, 1977; Cardinell, 1980; Leffingwell, 1979; Seyle, 1978; Weiskopf, 1980; Wey, 1951) are other manifestations which are reported in stress literature and research. Very often stressed teachers become indifferent and cynical or develop negative attitudes towards their students (Bardo, 1979; Cardinell, 1980; Freudenberger, 1977; Harrison, 1980; Leffingwell, 1979; Maslach, 1978; Walsh, 1979; Weiskopf, 1980). This often is manifested behaviorally. This particular behavioral manifestation of the stress-burnout process is distancing or withdrawing and a general loss of caring for the people (students) the stressed person works with on a daily basis. Moracco and McFadden have written:

> This distancing can be both emotional and physical. Emotional distancing includes developing a callous attitude toward students. Often, teachers experiencing stress refer to their students in demeaning ways. Expressions similar to 'You give them an inch and they take a mile' become common (1980, p. 11).

Other behavioral manifestations of the stress-burnout process are the following: an increase in absenteeism and/or general feeling of not wanting to go to work; a reluctance to attend department, faculty, and/or in-service meetings (Bardo, 1979; Harlin, 1976; Leffingwell, 1979; Moracco & McFadden, 1980; Walsh, 1979; Weiskopf, 1980); inadequate work performance; an increase in risk taking (Ban, 1980; Cardinell, 1980; Freudenberger, 1977; Moracco & McFadden, 1980); an increase in perspiration and "wringing of hands" (Leffingwell, 1979, p. 288); and an increase in alcohol and drug consumption (Cooper & Marshall, 1976; Harlin, 1976; Maslach, 1978; Moracco & McFadden, 1980; Walsh, 1979; Weiskopf, 1980). Becoming more inflexible, more rigid in thinking, and less compromising (Freudenberger, 1977) also are mentioned as behavioral manifestations.

Effects

The physiological, psychological, and behavioral effects of the stress-burnout process are well documented in the literature. They are closely associated with and are more prolonged than the stress-burnout manifestations (symptoms) previously mentioned. At times, however, the effects and symptoms are indistinguishable, and therefore cause an overlap in both the literature and this literature review. Stress effects vary in severity from feeling "run-down" and experiencing minor maladies (Alley, 1980; Cardinell, 1980; Freudenberger, 1977; Hendrickson, 1979; Moracco & McFadden, 1980; Walsh, 1979) to undergoing a total emotional breakdown (Hendrickson, 1979) and even to dying, the ultimate effect of the stress-burnout process (Alley, 1980).

Physically, the effects of the stress-burnout process attack all the major systems of the living human organism. In general, the stress-burnout process affects the cardiovascular system (Bloch, 1977, 1978; Kahn & Quinn, 1970; Margolis, Kroes, & Quinn, 1974; Muse, 1979, 1980); the respiratory system (Bloch, 1977, 1978); the immunological system (Muse, 1979, 1980); the skeletal-muscular system (Bloch, 1977, 1978; Muse, 1979, 1980); the genitourinary/digestive system (Bloch, 1978; Muse, 1979, 1980); the nervous system (Kahn & Quinn, 1970; Margolis et al., 1974; Walsh, 1979); and the endocrine system (Selye, 1976).

More specifically, the following systems of the body are affected by the stress-burnout process:

1. The cardiovascular system which can lead to:

    a. Heart palpitations, diseases, and attacks (Bloch, 1977, 1978; Harlin, 1976; Kahn & Quinn, 1970; Margolis et al., 1970; Muse, 1979, 1980; Newell, 1979; Selye, 1976; Walsh, 1979)

    b. Hypertension and associated high blood pressure problems (Berger, 1980; Bloch, 1977, 1978; CTU survey, 1978; Dale, 1976; G.E. Monogram, 1978; Harlin, 1976; Muse, 1979, 1980; Walley, 1978; Walsh, 1979)

2. The respiratory system which can lead to:

   a. Asthma and bronchial infections and related problems (Bloch, 1977, 1978; Cichon & Koff, 1978; G.E. Monogram, 1978; Harlin, 1976; Hendrickson, 1979; Newell, 1979; Walley, 1978)

   b. Hyperventilation (Bloch, 1977)

3. The immunological system which can lead to:

   a. Diabetes (Muse, 1979, 1980)

   b. Infections (Muse, 1979, 1980)

   c. Increased susceptibility to disease (Help! Teacher can't, 1980; Hendrickson, 1979)

   d. Cancer (Muse, 1980)

   e. Allergies and various skin disorders (Berger, 1980; Bloch, 1978; Muse, 1979, 1980; Walley, 1978)

4. The skeletal-muscular system which can lead to:

   a. Accident proneness and dizziness (Berger, 1980; Bloch, 1977; Help! Teacher can't, 1980; Hendrickson, 1979; Muse, 1979, 1980; Selye, 1976; Walley, 1978)

   b. Backaches (Bloch, 1977, 1978; Muse, 1979, 1980; Selye, 1976)

   c. Arthritis (Muse, 1979, 1980)

   d. Cervical tension (Bloch, 1977; Dale, 1976)

5. The genitourinary/digestive system which can lead to:

   a. Ulcers and various stomach disorder (Berger, 1980; Bloch, 1978; Harlin, 1976; Help! Teacher can't, 1980; Hendrickson, 1979; Muse, 1979, 1980; Newell, 1979; Selye, 1976; Walsh, 1979)

   b. Diarrhea or constipation (Bloch, 1978; Hendrickson, 1979; Muse, 1979, 1980; Selye, 1976)

   c. Colitus (Bloch, 1978; Dale, 1976; G.E. Monogram, 1978; Harlin, 1976; Hendrickson, 1979; Muse, 1979, 1980; Selye, 1976; Walsh, 1979)

   d. Renal disease and other kidney problems (G.E. Monogram, 1978; Newell, 1979; Selye, 1976; Walsh, 1979)

   e. Bladder problems (Berger, 1980)

   f. Menstrual irregularities and difficulties (Harlin, 1976; Selye, 1976)

6. The nervous system which can lead to:

   a. Headaches (including migraine, tension, and sinus) (Berger, 1980; Bloch, 1977, 1978; Harlin, 1976; Help! Teacher can't, 1980; Hendrickson, 1979; Kahn & Quinn, 1970; Margolis et al., 1978; Muse, 1979, 1980; Newell, 1979; Walley, 1978; Walsh, 1979)

   b. Seizures (Bloch, 1977)

c. Insomnia (CTU survey, 1978; Moracco & McFadden, 1980; Selye, 1976)

7. The endocrine system which can lead to:

a. Hormonal secretions which may be either helpful or dangerous to the human body (Selye, 1976)

The psychological effects of the stress-burnout process include the following: anxiety and severe depression (Berger, 1980; Bloch, 1977; G.E. Monogram, 1978; Harlin, 1976; Newell, 1979; Selye, 1976; Walley, 1978); debility and mental/physical fatigue (Berger, 1980; Bloch, 1977; Harlin, 1976; Hendrickson, 1979; Kahn & Quinn, 1970; National Association of Elementary Principals, 1980; Scrivens, 1979; Selye, 1976; Walley, 1978); low self-esteem and destruction of self-concept (Ban, 1980; Berger, 1980; Hendrickson, 1979; Walley, 1978); lack of sociability and increased and prolonged irritability (Bloch, 1977; Hendrickson, 1979; Selye, 1976; Walley, 1978; Walsh, 1979); heightened sensitivity to weather conditions (Bloch, 1977), schizophrenia (Harlin, 1976); and an over-all loss of will from which even suicidal tendencies may develop (Help! Teacher can't, 1980).

The behavioral effects of the stress-burnout process include an increasing number of teachers leaving the profession (Ban, 1980; McGuire, 1979; Muse, 1980; National Association of Elementary Principals, 1980); increased smoking, alcoholism, and drug addiction (Ban, 1980; Margolis et al., 1974; Newell, 1979; Selye, 1976); and frequent absenteeism and more failures on the job (Ban, 1980; Harlin, 1976; Kahn & Quinn, 1970; Walsh, 1979). The ultimate effect of the stress-burnout process is death (Alley, 1980; Selye, 1976).

The educational literature is filled with articles describing the burned out teacher in American schools, the effect upon children in the classroom, and the national tragedy which is developing. Stress has been singled out as a major cause and considerable time has been devoted to identifying the stresses contributing to the widespread malaise in schools (Cardinell, 1980, p. 9).

Coping Mechanisms

In order to prevent such malaise in the schools, teachers must learn how to cope with stress and its often deleterious effects. They must become aware of, learn, and even more important, utilize effective coping/controlling mechanisms. All too frequently people suffering from prolonged stress will resort to such negative coping mechanisms as increasing their intake of alcohol, which often leads to alcoholism, and/or increasing their usage of drugs (Broder, 1979; Cochrane & Robertson, 1973; Goodall & Brown, 1980; Selye, 1978). These techniques provide a temporary relief, and their consequences usually are more serious than those posited by the initiating problem.

The literature is replete with suggestions on how people can cope with stress. Pinpointing, identifying, and recognizing the source of stress is cited over and over as a most important stress controller (Collins, 1981; Goodall & Brown, 1980; Hendrickson, 1979; Kyriacou, 1981; Leffingwell, 1979; Weiskopf, 1980). Broder (1979), Goodall and Brown (1980), Harlin (1976), and Moe (1979) suggest that a person who is experiencing stress should be kind and good to himself/herself, for example, buy a new outfit, go to a movie, go out to dinner, etc. In other words, he/she deserves it! Others have suggested that people who are experiencing stress should do other "fun" activities, such as become involved in a hobby (Anderson, 1980; Broder, 1979; Goodall & Brown, 1980; Kyriacou, 1981; Moe, 1979; Weiskopf, 1980).

Getting away, taking a day off, going on a vacation, or even taking a leave of absence from teaching are other techniques suggested to help cope with stress (Alley, 1980; Calhoun, 1980; Kossack & Woods, 1980; Moe, 1979; Weiskopf, 1980). Weiskopf (1980) further suggests that people who are undergoing stress should avoid isolation, and should instead interact with people whom they consider to be fun and interesting to be around. Another suggestion is for stressed teachers to try to break up the amount of time of direct contact with their students by such measures as team teaching and establishing learning centers (Weiskopf, 1980). One who is experiencing stress in his/her life should avoid people and situations that are depressing and toxic (Collins, 1981; Goodall & Brown, 1980).

Physical exercise, such as isometrics and jogging, also is mentioned as an effective stress controller (Alley, 1980; Anderson, 1980; Broder, 1979; Bry, 1978; Cochrane & Robertson, 1973; Freudenberger, 1977; Harlin, 1976; Humphrey & Humphrey, 1980; Moe, 1979; Walker, 1975; Weiskopf, 1980). Establishing good eating and sleeping habits is essential to maintaining a healthy body and to preventing susceptibility to disease brought on by stress (Bloch, 1977; Broder, 1979; Calhoun, 1980; Collins, 1981; Harlin, 1976; Kossack & Woods, 1980; Moe, 1979). Learning effective relaxation techniques (deep breathing exercises, meditation, and yoga) is another effective way to cope with stress (Alley, 1980; Benson, 1975; Bry, 1978; Calhoun, 1980; Cochrane & Robertson, 1973; Cottler, 1978; Goodall & Brown, 1980; Leffingwell, 1979; Pelletier, 1977; Selye, 1978). Collins (1981) and Moe (1979) advise teachers not to feel guilty and/or worried about not being able to "reach" every student. They also suggest that teachers have to learn to say "no" to school administrators and supervisors, and that they can't allow people to "dump" everything (extracurricular activities) on them. Cichon and Koff (1978) advise teachers to attend stress reduction in-services (if available) with an open mind to help cope with their stress. Seeking professional help is a means teachers might use to help themselves cope (Broder, 1979; Dixon et al., 1980; Kossack & Woods, 1980).

Other coping mechanisms mentioned in the literature include the following:

1. Create or become a member of a support group to discuss stress commonalities (Alley, 1980; Broder, 1979; Calhoun, 1980; Collins, 1981; Freudenberger, 1977; Harlin, 1976; House approves, 1978; Kossack & Woods, 1980; Leffingwell, 1979; Maslach, 1978).

2. Develop good time management skills (Alley, 1980; Cochrance & Robertson, 1973; Collins, 1981; Kossack & Woods, 1980; Weiskopf, 1980).

3. Establish priorities by setting realistic goals. Learn to plan for success by analyzing and working things out. Be prepared by understanding your strengths and weaknesses (Alley, 1980; Bloch, 1977; Broder, 1979; Collins, 1981; Freudenberger, 1977; Kossack & Woods, 1980; Kyriacou, 1981; Moe, 1979).

4. Get in "touch" with your feelings by maintaining a diary or journal. Record those stressors which upset you and note why you think they do (Hendrickson, 1979; Moe, 1979).

5. Learn to separate home and school problems. Leave school problems at school, and home problems at home (Alley, 1980; Anderson, 1980; Broder, 1979; Collins, 1981; Kyriacou, 1981; Maslach, 1978).

6. Dress up or improve the facilities where you work--your classroom, the faculty lounge. All too often the work

environment is drab and dreary (Kossack & Woods, 1980).

7. Utilize biofeedback techniques (Benson, 1975; Brown, 1974, 1977; Calhoun, 1980; Cochrane & Robertson, 1973; Pelletier, 1977).

Is there any specific coping mechanism or formula of several controllers of stress which could guarantee stress reduction for all human beings? In discussing this concern, Selye writes:

> It must be clearly understood that there is no ready-made success formula which would suit everybody. We are all different. The only thing we have in common is our obedience to certain fundamental biologic laws which govern all men. I think the best the professional investigator of stress can do is to explain the mechanism of stress as far as he can understand it; then, to outline the way he thinks this knowledge could be applied to problems or daily life; and, finally, as a kind of laboratory demonstration to describe the way he himself applied it successfully to his own problem (1976, p. 454).

Specifically addressing the problem of teacher stress Needle, Griffin, and Svendsen say:

> The question is how teachers cope with problems and job pressures which occur regularly rather than in isolated situations and which impact on a wide range of teachers. . . .
> Specific coping responses -behaviors, cognitions, and perceptions -inform us about some of the things teachers do to deal with stress on the job. The question of how effective these coping strategies are in reducing stress has only begun to be addressed by researchers (1981, p. 178).

Special Education Teachers and Stress

The primary focus of this study was to investigate special education teachers' perceptions of stress as compared with those of regular classroom teachers. Previously mentioned was the fact that very little research on stress as related to teachers of special education students has been reported in the literature. However, the area of concern has not been totally ignored. Weiskopf (1980) most directly addresses the issue of stress and "teachers of exceptional children" (p. 18). Although she does not support her claim with empirical data, she states, "It is distressingly apparent that teachers in general and special educators in particular are burning out on the job" (p. 18). She addresses the issue that teacher burnout is not selective and that "the problems of teacher burnout . . . extend beyond the teacher by also affecting students, school staff, parents, and the teacher's family" (p. 18). Teacher burnout is not selective also because it affects teachers at all educational levels and settings. The focus of the Weiskopf article is the description of the stress-burnout process on special education teachers at the elementary and secondary levels, including regular classroom teachers who have special education students mainstreamed into their classes and teachers of special day classes. "These teachers work closely and intensely with children who require constant care, support, and supervision" (pp. 18-19). With the possible exception that teachers of exceptional children may have the additional stressor of working with children who have special needs, the stress-burnout process parallels the process for other teachers. The symptoms, effects, coping mechanisms, and suggestions for burnout prevention are identical to those reported in the literature for teachers in general. Weiskopf contends that the difference is that the stressed special education teacher more adversely affects his/her students. "At worst, since exceptional children usually lack the ego strength of regular children, a cynical, negative teacher could seriously impair their progress academically and socially" (Weiskopf, 1980, p. 22).

Dixon, Shaw, and Bensky (1980) investigated the role the school administrator should undertake to prevent burnout among teachers as it relates to the implementation of Public Law 94-142. They report that the degree of burnout within a school system is "directly related to the degree of stress experienced by individual staff members and by the special services organization as a whole" (p. 30).

D'Alonzo and Wiseman (1978) see role ambiquity as a major determiner of job dissatisfaction for the high school learning disability resource teacher. They suggest that the high school learning disability resource teacher (special education teacher) must be the following:

1. A teacher who must be among the best.
2. A curriculum specialist with a comprehensive understanding of a variety of subject areas.
3. An expert in methods of working with students who are difficult to instruct and reach.
4. A technician competent in the use of the "tools of the trade," both hardware and software.
5. An administrator who keeps reports, records, and arranges schedules of others.
6. A counselor who deals first-hand with educational, social, occupational, and personal problems.
7. A public and human relations expert in working and communicating with administrators, colleagues, students, and parents.
8. A diagnostician whose competence plays a major part in student learning (p. 63).

Often the functions of the high school learning disability resource teacher are not appreciated and sometimes are forgotten by school administrators, other teachers, and parents. These functions must not be ignored either by the aforementioned persons or by representatives of state departments of education, and local school boards of education. The behavior and effectiveness of these special education teachers, as well as other professionals, are determined by role expectations, both theirs and those of others.

> The data appear to indicate that the role of the secondary learning disability teacher is not generally agreed on or defined . . . . A clear trend does exist, however, indicating that secondary resource teachers do want to be more involved in the total program for the secondary learning disabled student . . . . The marked difference between actual performance and desired performance indicates that resource teachers are not performing the roles they feel are most needed (D'Alonzo & Wiseman, 1978, p. 69).

Instruments Used In Stress Studies

The review of the literature has identified several instruments which have been utilized in teacher stress research. Most of the data gathering instruments employed have been self-report, "pencil-paper," structured questionnaires. Although a variety of instruments have been used in stress studies, Clark (1980) reports that there are no adequate instruments devised to ascertain teachers' perceptions of stress "when compared with a variety of demographic variables" (p. 6). In their attempt to assess the mental health of teachers, Bentz, Holister, and Edgerton (1971) employed the Health Opinion Survey which was developed in 1957 by MacMillan and was later refined in 1963 by Leighton and his colleagues. This questionnaire is a 20 item survey which is primarily psychophysiological in nature. "Its underlying rationale is that disorder is reflected in behaviors indicative of reactions to stress that anyone can register upon question" (Bentz et al., 1971, p. 73). When comparing the mental health of teachers with the mental health of community leaders and the general public, the researchers report that the "overall mental health among the teachers and the community leaders appears to be better than that of the general public" (Bentz et al., 1971, p. 76). The Minnesota Multiphasic Personality Inventory (MMPI) and projective tests have been utilized by Bloch during the several years he has devoted to studying battered teachers. The results of his research have indicated that teachers are "obsessional, passive, idealistic, dedicated persons, who are unable to understand or cope with violence directed toward them" (Bloch, 1977, p. 62).

In 1967 Holmes and Rahe developed the Social Readjustment Rating Scale (SRRS). This instrument consists of 43 items which represent most of the common life events which require change in social adjustment. "The majority of research concerned with life event stress has made use of the Social Readjustment Rating Scale" (Cichon & Koff, 1978, p. 1). Each item on the questionnaire is awarded a certain "weight" as determined by the item's degree of necessary readjustment. "For example, death of a spouse is weighted at 100 (the highest point on the scale), marriage at 50, change in recreation at 19, vacation at 12" (Cichon & Koff, 1978, p. 1). Since its development in 1967, a variety of modified forms of the SRRS have been developed for use in studies concerned with specific populations and life events which are common to these particular groups (children, athletes, college students, etc.).

With the cooperation of a committee of teachers from the Chicago Teachers Union (CTU), Cichon and Koff developed the Teaching Stress Events Inventory (TSEI). This instrument is another modification of the SRRS since it includes appropriate items from the original instrument developed by Holmes and Rahe (1967). The researchers and the committee from the CTU developed a 36 item inventory of events common to teaching. In November, 1977, via the monthly issue of the CTU newsletter, 22,448 TSEI surveys were distributed. The researchers received 4,934 usable questionnaires for analysis purposes. This represents approximately 22% of the 22,448 teachers employed by the Chicago Board of Education at the time when the study was the conducted. Results of the Cichon and Koff research are previously mentioned in this text, and they are significant, for their research represents a major effort in investigating teacher stress.

Dale (1977) used four instruments in her study concerned with gathering empirical data "on the relationship of stress provoking aspects of the administrative role and the presence of selected risk factors in coronary heart disease" (p. 6169-A).

The first instrument, Biographical Information, was used to gather data about medical conditions for which the respondents were currently receiving treatment. The second instrument, the Stressful Situation Scale, was used to collect data about the number of stressful situations the respondents recently had experienced. The third instrument, the Percieved Occupational Stress Scale, was designed by Dr. Robert L. Kahn and his associates at the University of Michigan. The scale was used with the permission of Dr. Kahn, and measured the amount of stress the administrative personnel felt. The fourth instrument, the Behavioral Risk Factor Analysis, was used to obtain data about the daily activities of the respondents that may have caused a pre-disposition to coronary heart disease (Dale, 1977, p. 6169-A).

Another study concerned with stress and school administrative personnel was conducted in the Fort Wayne Community Schools, Fort Wayne, Indiana (Baugh, 1977). The instrument used in this study was the School Administrator Stress Survey, an 84 item instrument which was submitted to 260 school administrators. The Manifest Anxiety Scale (MAS), developed by Taylor in 1953, was selected by Doyal and Forsyth (1973) to measure teachers' general anxiety level. "The 50 items on the MAS were chosen for their ability to detect clinical anxiety" (Doyal & Forsyth, 1973, p. 232). Employing the Test Anxiety Questionnaire developed by Mandler and Saracon in 1952, Koon (1971) examined the effects of teacher anxiety and teacher expectations in teacher-pupil interaction (cited in Coates & Thoresen, 1976, p. 169).

Other instruments used in teacher stress and/or anxiety research include the following: the Flanders Interaction Analysis (Gustafson, 1969); the IPAT Anxiety Scale (Gustafson, 1969); the Minnesota Teacher Attitude Inventory and the Rokeach Dogmatism Scale (Hughes, 1970); the State-Trait Anxiety Inventory (Eder, 1971) (cited in Coates & Thoresen, 1976, pp. 173-174).

Since the TOSFQ had been designed to measure teachers' perceptions of occupational stress factors, it was the instrument chosen to be utilized in this study. Permission was received from Clark to use the 30 item TOSFQ to identify perceptions of occupational stressors. Additional sections also were included. These will be discussed in detail in a subsequent chapter.

The Teacher Occupational Stress Factor Questionnaire (TOSFQ) is a 30 item self-report questionnaire, which was constructed, scaled, and validated by Clark (1980). The TOSFQ is a five factor data-gathering instrument specifically developed to identify the perceived occupational stress factors of teachers (Clark, 1980, pp. 138-141). The questionnaire's original 97 likert-type stimulus items were factor analyzed according to the principal components method after its initial administration of 391 Georgia classroom teachers. "Both Kaiser's Varimax and oblique rotations were executed" (Clark, 1980, p. v) with the oblique solution proving to be "the best linear fit of the data" (Clark, 1980, p. v). Five factors and 30 items (each loading at least ± .55) emerged.

A random sample of 400 Alabama teachers cross-validated the factored questionnaire on which a second factor analysis was completed. Results of this analysis indicated job-induced stress as perceived by teachers in a multidimensional concept composed of five factors: (1) feeling of professional inadequacy; (2) principal-teacher professional relationships; (3) collegial relationships; (4) group instruction; and (5) job overload.

The two administrations of the TOSFQ on the two different samples extracted considerable variance. Because of this, Clark concluded "that the factors have high reliability and do, in fact, define the dimensions of the concept of job-induced stress as perceived by teachers" (Clark, 1980, p. 74).

A communality estimate comparison across the first administration (Georgia) and second administration (Alabama) revealed "that the items were consistently interrelated" (Clark, 1980, p. 82). A comparison of eigenvalues across both administrations confirmed that the data contained five strong factors and "validated the fact that the questionnaire tapped the dimensionality of perceived teacher job-induced stress" (Clark, 1980, p. 84).

Cronbach's coefficient alpha was computed to examine the internal consistency of the five factors. The internal consistency for Factor 1 was .937; Factor 2 was .982; Factor 3 was .958; Factor 4 was .936; and Factor 5 was .933 (Clark, 1980, p. 88). The high magnitudes of the internal consistency of the scales are apparent from the information reported in Table 1.

Table 1

Internal Consistency Coefficients
For Each Of The Five Factors

Factor	Internal Consistency
1 - Professional Inadequacy	.937
2 - Principal/Teacher Professional Relationships	.982
3 - Collegial Relationships	.958
4 - Group Instruction	.936
5 - Job Overload	.933

Note. From "An Analysis of Occupational Stress Factors as Perceived by Public School Teachers" by E. H. Clark. Unpublished doctoral dissertation, Auburn University, 1980, p. 88.

Summary of the Review of Literature

The amount of research reported in the literature concerning teacher stress lends support for the need to investigate this phenomenon more closely. From the literature it was noted that the lack of research concerning the special education teacher and stress mandates the urgency of research in this specific area of teacher stress.

Various definitions of stress have been presented. The Moracco and McFadden (1980) definition of stress, emphasizing an alteration of psychological homeostasis, accompanying physiological changes, perception mediation, threats to self esteem, as well as incorporating the appraisal process, was chosen as the definition of teacher stress for this study. In an attempt to present a systematic approach to the study of stress in the teaching profession, compatible with the chosen definition of stress, an interactional model of stress was presented. (See Figure 1.)

The severity and variety of the symptoms and effects of teacher stress have been addressed, together with the associated positive and negative coping mechanisms. Weiskopf (1980) addressed the issue of stress and the special education teacher--one of the two research questions of this investigation. Specifically, that question unanswered in the literature is: "Do special education teachers perceive stress differently from other classroom teachers?" The second research question, "Do the stated demographic variables affect teachers' perceptions of stress?" was addressed in the review.

Although the amount of research concerned with stress in the teaching profession has increased in the last few years, it is still in its early stages of development. A need for more "field research" in the area of teacher stress and especially in the area of stress and the special education teacher beckons all of us interested in maintaining educational quality.

III. METHODS

Introduction

Chapter III is divided into six sections. The first section describes the setting where the study was conducted. The description of the setting is presented in specific language to help the reader better understand and appreciate the type of setting where the study took place.

The second section of Chapter III describes the sample of the study. The third section delineates the five sections of the modified TOSFQ used in the present study. The fourth section describes the procedures which were employed to collect data for this investigation. The fifth section, Design of the Study, explains the descriptive research approach of this investigation. The final section of Chapter III states the statistical procedures used to analyze the data.

Method

Setting

The setting for the study was a large school system, one of the the fifteen largest school systems in the country, with a student enrollment approximating 121,000 students. Geographically, it is located in close proximity to Washington, D.C.

At the beginning of the 1980-1981 school year, the school system had more than 215 public school facilities, including 144 elementary schools (grades kindergarten-6), one middle school (grades 7-8), 40 junior high schools (grades 7-9), 17 senior high schools (grades 10-12), two high schools (grades 9-12), 10 special education centers (ungraded), one vocational education center (grades 10-12), and one special education vocational center (grades 9-12).

The county school system is divided into three administrative areas, each of which is directed by an area assistant superintendent. The three areas (northern, southern, and central) have been divided according to administrative rationale only. It can be assumed that the "make-up" of any one of the three areas would be fairly representative of the other two in terms of population, socio-economic status, and the educational quality of the schools.

Since it was administratively unfeasible to attempt to coordinate a research study including all three areas, the central administrative area was selected as the area in which this study would be conducted. There is no reason to believe that the findings of this study could not be logically generalized to the northern and southern administrative areas of the county.

The almost 500 square mile county where the study was conducted has characteristics which are common to other large metropolitan school systems. There are areas in the county which could easily be identified as suburban, rural, or urban. All three administrative areas include these similar demographic characteristics. Similar to most metropolitan areas across the country, this county has one chief industry and several other sources of revenue for its citizenry. The difference, however, is that the chief industry of this county is the United States Government. A large percentage of the county's residents are directly employed by the federal government, or indirectly earn their incomes from industries which owe their service related existences to the vast bureaucracy of the federal government. Other county industries include farming (chiefly tobacco), horse raising, limited manufacturing, and transportation.

The system is and has been experiencing many of the same problems plaguing other school systems across the nation. In a period of less than six years, the student enrollment has declined by more than 14,000 students, and the 1983 school year projection is that the enrollment will be reduced by another 22,000 students. The declining student enrollment has affected the school system's staffing. In a one-year period, from the 1979-1980 school year to the 1980-1981 school year, the professional staff was reduced by some 400 positions. Similar reductions also have occurred among the classified or non-professional staff. Accountability demands, inflation, and the increasingly austere budgets also have taken their tolls. Despite these phenomena, the system's budget of approximately $300,000,000 authorized an expenditure of more than $2,000 per non-special education student, approximately $200 above the national average in per pupil expenditure (N.E.A., 1979, p. 47). More than $6,000 was spent on each of the approximately 15,000 special education students, who had been so identified and enrolled in special education classes and programs throughout the school system.

The school system has one of the largest and most respected special education programs in the country. It employs almost 1,300 special education professional personnel and special education aides. Special education programs are available in the three administrative areas of the county, pre-school through high school, and are available in each county public school. Special education centers are provided for children with more severe multiple handicapping conditions. A program also is provided by the county public school system for students who are unable to attend school for extended periods of time.

Sample

The total population for this study was comprised of the approximately 6,000 classroom teachers (regular and special education teachers) included in the entire school system. The accessible population consisted of the classroom teachers employed in the central administrative area, or approximately 1/3 of the total teacher population of the county school system.

The sample for this study consisted of 1,335 elementary, middle, junior high, senior high, high school, and special center teachers. Both regular classroom teachers and special education teachers were included.

The schools included in the sample were identified (coded) in the in the following manner:

1. Elementary Schools (k-6)--Coded as 100-123
2. Middle School (6-8)--Coded as 200
3. Junior High Schools--(7-9) Coded as 300-312
4. High School (9-12)--Coded as 400
5. Senior High Schools--Coded as 500-503
6. Special Education Centers (Ungraded) and the Special Education Vocational Center (9-12)--Coded as 600-604

Of the 691 respondents, 195 (28.2%) subjects identified themselves as male teachers; 475 (68.7%) subjects identified themselves as female teachers, and 21 (3.1%) subjects failed to respond to this item of the survey. The sample included 148 (21.4%) single teachers, 477 (69.0%) married teachers, 53 (7.7%) divorced teachers, nine (1.3%) widowed teachers, and four (.5%) teachers who did not respond to this survey item. Demographic information explaining the racial compositon of the sample is provided in Table 4.

These data are reported in Table 2.

Table 2

Surveyed Schools By Series Identification, Number of Teachers Surveyed, Number of Respondents, and Respondent Percentage for Each School

Code	Teachers	Return	Percentage
100	17	7	41.1
101	21	20	95.2
103	23	11	47.8
104	22	15	68.2
105	22	8	36.4
106	24	17	70.8
107	9	5	55.6
108	13	11	84.6
109	20	5	25.0
110	21	13	61.9
111	18	11	61.1
112	23	8	34.8
113	22	4	18.2
114	18	15	83.3
115	12	5	41.7
116	22	9	40.9
117	18	12	66.6
118	16	8	50.0

Table 2 (Continued)

Surveyed Schools By Series
Identification, Number of Teachers Surveyed,
Number of Respondents, and
Respondent Percentage for Each School

Code	Teachers	Return	Percentage
119	20	9	45.0
120	30	12	40.0
121	17	12	70.6
122	14	12	85.7
123	20	5	25.0
200	30	6	20.0
300	41	17	41.5
301	24	12	50.0
302	34	26	76.5
303	40	6	15.0
304	29	16	55.2
305	33	28	84.8
306	30	10	33.3
307	27	10	37.0
308	37	27	72.9
309	44	29	65.9
310	32	23	71.9
311	22	4	18.2

Table 2 (Continued)

Surveyed Schools By Series
Identification, Number of Teachers Surveyed,
Number of Respondents, and
Respondent Percentage for Each School

Code	Teachers	Return	Percentage
312	40	26	65.0
400	84	36	42.8
500	114	65	57.0
501	55	21	38.2
502	75	19	25.3
503	NEVER DISTRIBUTED TO STAFF		
600	13	9	69.2
601	11	10	90.0
602	11	11	100.0
603	27	15	41.7
604	24	22	91.7
Totals	1,335	691	51.76

The following demographic data are provided in Table 3 to help the reader better understand the age composition of the sample.

Table 3

Age of Sampled Teachers

Age Group	Number of Respondents	Respondent Percentage
21-30	160	23.2
31-40	284	41.1
41-50	145	21.0
51-60	57	8.2
61 and older	12	1.7
Missing Cases	33	4.8
Totals	691	100.0

From the teachers who answered, 294 (42.5%) had earned their B.S. or B.A. Degrees; 377 (54.6%) had earned their Masters of Science or Education Degrees; eight (1.2%) subjects had earned their Specialist in Education Degrees, and eight (1.2%) had earned their doctorate degrees. There were four (.6%) missing cases for this item. Years of teaching experience of the sample are reported in Table 5.

Respondents were asked to identify themselves as either special education teachers or non special education teachers. From the reporting teachers, 130 (18.8%) subjects identified themselves as special education teachers, and 542 (78.4%) reported that they were not special education teachers. There were 19 (2.8%) missing cases for this item. Teachers included in the survey were asked to delineate the school type in which they were currently teaching. These data are illustrated in Table 6.

Table 4

Racial Composition of Sampled Teachers

Race	Number of Respondents	Respondent Percentage
Caucasian	523	75.7
Black	131	19.0
Spanish Surname	15	2.2
Asian	4	.6
Other	11	1.6
Missing Cases	7	1.0
Totals	691	100.0

Respondents were requested to characterize their school settings as either rural, suburban, or urban. Based on personal, individual choice, 11 (1.6%) of the responding teachers said their school setting was rural; 599 (86.7%) reported their school setting was suburban, and 74 (10.7%) stated that they taught in an urban school setting. For this particular item there were seven (1.0%) missing cases. School enrollment data (number of students) are reported in Table 7.

Of the responding teachers, 455 (65.8%) subjects worked in schools having male principals, and 221 (32.0%) subjects worked in schools having female principals. There were 15 (2.2%) missing cases for this item.

Table 5

Years of Teaching Experience of Sampled Teachers

Experience in Years	Number of Respondents	Respondent Percentage
1-5	105	15.2
6-10	207	30.0
11-15	184	26.6
16-20	109	15.8
21 or More	80	11.6
Missing Cases	6	.9
Totals	691	100.0[*]

[*]Note. Total may not equal 100% due to rounding error.

Instrumentation

Much already has been reported concerning the constructing and scaling of the TOSFQ developed by Clark (1980) which provided the basis for the survey instrument used in this study. To this date, the TOSFQ has not been used in any other research studies except the two initial studies in Georgia and Alabama. Also, this is the first study using a modified TOSFQ. The modification of the instrument used in the present investigation consisted of Clark's 30 Likert-type items plus three additional data collection sections, and one demographic data collection section. The first 30 items of the 99 item questionnaire used in this study comprise Clark's 1980 TOSFQ. These first 30 items are Section 1 of the questionnaire used in this study.

Table 6

Type of School

School Type	Number of Respondents	Respondent Percentage
Elementary (K-6)	235	34.0
Middle (7-8)/Junior (7-9)	243	35.2
High School (9-12)	69	10.0
Senior High (10-12)	78	11.3
Special Education Center	63	9.1
Missing Cases	3	.4
Totals	691	100.0

As mentioned earlier in this text, Clark's TOSFQ consists of five factors. These factors include the following: (1) Professional Inadequacy, (2) Principal/Teacher Professional Relationships, (3) Collegial Relationships, (4) Group Instruction, and (5) Job Overload. The internal consistency range of the factors includes a low scale of .933 for Factor 5 to a high score of .982 for Factor 2. For further clarification refer to Table 1, the Internal Consistency Coefficients for Each of the Five Factors, mentioned in Chapter II.

The second section of the instrument used in this study was concerned with teachers' feelings about themselves and their students. This section was designed to determine the Obsessive-Compulsive Ideations and the Teacher Belief Systems of the teachers who participated in the study. The included section items (31-50) also were Likert-type in far as teachers were asked to respond as to how strongly they agreed or disagreed with each statement. The range of choices included the

Table 7

School Enrollment

Number of Students	Number of Respondents	Respondent Percentage
Less than 200	70	10.1
200-400	136	19.7
400-600	141	20.4
600-800	134	19.4
More than 800	207	30.0
Missing Cases	3	.4
Totals	691	100.0

following: (A) strongly agree; (B) agree; (C) neutral; (D) disagree; and (E) strongly disagree. Specifically, Items 31-40 were concerned with how teachers feel about their students.

Items 41-50 are concerned with people's beliefs and feelings about themselves. These items were constructed by Burns (1980, p. 44), and were included to collect data to reveal the degree of perfectionism or nonperfectionism of the teachers surveyed.

Section 3 (items 51-72) of the questionnaire used in this study was concerned with commom symptoms of stress as reported in the literature. Teachers were requested to respond to the frequency with which they have experienced each of the 22 common symptoms of stress which were listed. The range of choices included the following: (A) never; (B) rarely; (C) sometimes; (D) often; and (E) always.

Section 4 (items 73-84) of the questionnaire was concerned with how teachers cope with stress. Teachers were asked to report the frequency with which they used the listed coping mechanisms to relax. The range of choices included the following: (A) never; (B) rarely; (C) sometimes; (D) often; and (E) always. Item 84 asked teachers to report the frequency with which they used some other common measure to relax. Respondents were not asked to identify what this measure was.

Section 5 (items 85-99) was concerned with collecting demographic information. The demographic data collected in this section are reported elsewhere in this chapter.

Procedures

In October, 1980, the researcher asked the Supervisor of Research and Development of a suburban Washington, D. C., school system about the possibility of conducting a research study in that system. The supervisor expressed an interest in the study and offered his cooperation. The school system's application form to conduct research was forwarded to the researcher, completed, and returned to the system. Permission was granted to conduct the study. At this point the researcher was advised to contact the Assistant Superintendent of schools for the Central Administrative Area of the system. The assistant superintendent was very cooperative and provided encouragement and support.

The central area of the county school system includes 48 elementary schools, one middle school, 13 junior high schools, one high school, four senior high schools, and five special education centers, including one special education vocational school. Of the 48 elementary schools, it was jointly decided between representatives of the school system and the researcher's doctoral advisory committee to randomly select 24 elementary schools (50%) to participate in the study. All other schools in this administrative area would be provided the opportunity to participate.

The researcher contacted the building principals of the 24 elementary schools and the other central area schools to determine their interest in permitting their teachers (regular classroom and special education) to participate in the study. Although the Central Area Assistant Superintendent provided the researcher with a letter of introduction stating her support for the study, it was made clear that each building principal would be given the choice to allow or not allow the study to be conducted in his/her particular school. It was further understood that participation by teachers was to be voluntary and anonymous. Two of the randomly selected elementary schools' principals did not permit the study to be conducted in their schools and subsequently two other elementary schools had to be randomly selected. All other building principals gave permission for the study to be conducted.

The researcher adhered to the school system's request that the surveys be distributed in the manner selected by and most convenient to the principal of each participating school. Two methods of distributing the surveys to teaching staffs emerged. Principals either placed the surveys in teachers' mail boxes with an announcement to return them at their convenience or by a particular date, or distribute them at a faculty meeting and again asked teachers to return the forms at their convenience or by a particular date. In all instances the teachers were advised that their participation in the study was voluntary and that there was no reason to reveal their identities. The instructions to the teachers were that they were participating in a research study concerned with teacher stress.

Arrangements were made with each building principal to have the researcher retrieve completed questionnaires. Due to internal administrative problems, one senior high school never was able to distribute the questionnaires to its staff and had to be omitted from the sample. Returns ranging from 15% to 100% were received from participating schools. (Refer to Table 2.)

All responses were placed on Auburn University General Purpose Scan Forms. No responses were made on the questionnaires. After all the scan forms had been collected, they were returned to Auburn for coding and analysis purposes. The researcher was successful in collecting 691 usable answer sheets of the 1,335 distributed questionnaires and answer sheets for a response rate of 51.76%.

Design of the Study

The study utilized a descriptive research approach to obtain the data. According to educational researchers, this type of research is designed for the purpose of obtaining information concerning the status of a current phenomenon (Ary, Jacobs, & Razavieh, 1972, p. 286).

Lehmann and Mehrens concur: "Descriptive research ... is concerned with the nature and degree of existing conditions" (1971, p. 95). The aim of descriptive research studies of this type is to determine the "nature of a situation as it exists at the time of the study. There is no administration or control of a treatment as is found in experimental research" (Ary et al., 1972, p. 286). In this inquiry, the phenomenon of teacher stress was investigated; more specifically, the investigation focused upon teachers' (regular and special education) perceptions of occupational stress factors.

The study was designed and conducted not only to collect data on the present condition of teacher stress, but also to obtain information on how these stress data are related to the stated demographic variables. This type of descriptive research, which enables the investigator to determine the degree to which variations of variables are related, frequently is referred to as a correlational study (Ary et al., 1972).

The variables of particular interest to the investigation included the following: Marital Status, Years Teaching Experience, Sex of Principal, Special Education (vs. Regular Classroom Experience), Teacher Belief Systems, Obsessive-Compulsive Ideations, Type of School, and School Setting.

Analyses of the Data

Teachers' scores on the modified TOSFQ were analyzed utilizing both descriptive and inferential statistical tests. Multiple regression and factor analysis techniques were included in these tests. Demographic data also were analyzed to ascertain whether there were differences on each of the selected variables for the sample.

IV. RESULTS

The findings of the investigation are presented in Chapter IV, Results. The chapter is divided into four sections. The first section is concerned with the effect that stress has on teacher absenteeism. Items 96-99 on the modified TOSFQ addressed this phenomenon (See Appendix B). The second section of Chapter IV compares the results of factor analysis procedures on Clark's TOSFQ and on the responses to the TOSFQ used in the current inquiry. The third section delineates the results of the regression analyses of the predictor variables of teacher stress. Specifically, the variables were Special Education (versus regular) Teachers' perceptions of stress (Hypothesis$_1$), School Setting (Hypothesis$_2$), Type of School (Hypothesis$_3$), Sex of Principal (Hypothesis$_4$), Marital Status (Hypothesis$_5$), Years of Teaching Experience (Hypothesis$_6$), Teacher Belief Systems (Hypothesis$_7$), and Obsessive-Compulsive Ideations of teachers (Hypothesis$_8$). This last section summarizes the results and tests the eight hypotheses of the study.

Teacher Absenteeism and Stress

The 691 respondents were requested to estimate the number of days they were absent from work during September through December, 1980. Nearly 75% of the respondents claimed between one and seven days of absenteeism. Additionally, 20% of the respondents claimed they were absent from work eight or more days. These data are reported in Table 8.

Teachers also were asked to report if, in their opinion, stress was a factor in the number of working days they were absent. From the 691 responding teachers, 296 (42.8%) said that stress was a factor, and 384 (55.6%) stated that stress was not a factor. There were 11 (1.6%) missing

Table 8

Number of School Days Missed
As Reported by Respondents

School Days Missed	Number of Respondents	Respondent Percentage
None (0)	44	6.4
1-3	214	31.0
4-7	293	42.4
8-11	92	13.3
12 or More	47	6.8
Missing Cases	1	0.1
Totals	691	100.0

cases. Teachers reporting absence from school because of stress were further requested to estimate this absenteeism percentage (item 98). This information is reported in Table 9.

About 51% ($n = 346$) of the teachers responded to item 98, though only 42.8% ($n = 296$) related that stress was a factor in their absenteeism (item 97). Approximately 50% of the 346 responding teachers reported that 20% to 50% of their absenteeism was due to stress. It was decided to use $n = 346$ even though some respondents may not have answered in the affirmative to item 97.

The response to the last demographic item of the survey, "If you had your life to live over, would you become a teacher?," revealed that 330 (47.8%) teachers said "yes," and 354 (51.2%) said they would not become teachers. There were seven (1.0%) missing cases for this item.

Table 9

Estimate of Percentage of Work Days Missed
Due To Stress by 346 Respondents

Estimate of Percentage of Days Due to Stress	Number of Respondents	Percentage Response to Item
10	101	29.2
20	79	22.8
50	92	26.6
70	41	11.8
90	33	9.5
Totals	346	100.0*

*Note. Total may not equal 100% due to rounding error.

Comparison of Factor Analysis Procedures

  Factor analysis is a much more generalized procedure for locating and defining dimensional space among a relatively large group of variables. Because of the generality of factor analysis, it is difficult to present a capsule description of its functions and applications. The major use of factor analysis by social scientists is to locate a smaller number of valid dimensions, clusters, or factors contained in a larger set of independent items or variables. And viewed from the other side, factor analysis can help determine the degree to which a given variable or several variables are part of a common underlying phenomenon (Nie, Hull, Jenkins, Steinbrenner, & Bent, 1975, p. 10).

In the process of cross validating the TOSFQ, Clark (1980) discovered that the oblique rotation factor analysis procedure proved to be the best fit for the variables on the five factors. These factors include the following: Professional Inadequacy (items 1, 2, 9, 14, 19, 25, and 28); Principal/Teacher Professional Relationships (items 3, 7, 10, 15, 17, 20, and 26); Collegial Relationships (items 4, 8, 11, 18, 23, 27, and 30); Group Instruction (items 5, 12, 16, 21, and 24); and Job Overload (items 6, 13, 22, and 29). The oblique rotation eliminated overloadings and reduced the instrument to 30 items. The five emerging factors accounted for 77.3% of the total variance (Clark, 1980, p. 110). An oblique factor analysis also was performed on the responses to the first 30 items (the original TOSFQ) used in the present study. A comparison of these data is reported in Table 10.

The oblique rotation performed on the responses to the TOSFQ used in this study resulted in items 3, 7, 10, 15, 17, 20, and 26 loading in Factor 1 renamed "Administrative Support." Items 1, 5, 9, 12, 19, 21, 24, and 25 loaded in Factor 2 renamed "Working With Students." Items 2, 14, and 28 loaded in Factor 3 renamed "Financial Security." Items 4, 8, 11, 18, 23, 27, and 30 loaded in Factor 4 renamed "Relationships With Teachers." Items 6, 13, 16, 22, and 29 loaded in Factor 5 renamed "Task Overload." The aforementioned data are illustrated in Table 11.

Table 10

Oblique Rotation Comparisons of Clark's TOSFQ and
Present TOSFQ's First 30 Items

	Clark's TOSFQ Loadings					Present TOSFQ Loadings				
		Factors					Factors			
Item	1	2	3	4	5	1	2	3	4	5
1	.761	.063	.073	.092	.001	.012	.560	-.028	-.079	-.066
2	.936	.020	.023	.085	.002	.000	-.022	-.915	-.029	.026
3	.008	.966	.006	.027	.000	.776	-.008	-.055	-.055	.014
4	.062	.042	.927	.048	.024	.183	.029	.058	.615	.094
5	.060	.055	.003	.894	.038	-.053	.662	.039	-.036	-.048
6	.062	.026	.017	.023	.882	.021	-.037	-.054	.009	-.715
7	.003	.963	.013	.004	.019	.853	.024	-.016	-.014	.006
8	.030	.018	.792	.010	.073	.062	-.035	-.090	.475	-.063
9	.778	.086	.028	.063	.019	-.062	.440	-.177	.207	-.011
10	.030	.955	.029	.015	.044	.773	.037	.019	.047	-.035
11	.009	.009	.903	.016	.055	.053	.012	.051	.721	.031
12	.005	.108	.025	.870	.059	-.085	.602	-.078	-.049	-.176
13	.014	.009	.038	.011	.880	.192	.111	-.067	-.059	-.539
14	.925	.028	.059	.085	.019	.035	-.005	-.958	-.007	.012
15	.012	.969	.052	.021	.011	.653	.035	-.043	.077	.016
16	.006	.007	.010	.851	.036	-.031	.312	.017	-.022	-.437
17	.022	.872	.041	.032	.023	.436	.050	-.103	.217	-.139
18	.017	.018	.917	.009	.025	-.002	.035	.024	.888	.064
19	.560	.008	.017	.213	.075	-.017	.695	-.066	.022	-.035
20	.039	.922	.009	.022	.016	.777	.008	.024	-.004	-.089
21	.076	.044	.004	.863	.070	.082	.679	.056	.049	-.011
22	.018	.033	.037	.015	.833	.069	-.020	-.017	.079	-.577
23	.060	.083	.832	.001	.033	.037	.055	-.069	.485	-.165
24	.020	.116	.046	.820	.029	.167	.651	.090	.036	.133
25	.788	.018	.067	.035	.007	.045	.508	-.141	.143	-.015
26	.001	.950	.003	.009	.009	.812	-.041	-.026	.022	-.020
27	.031	.024	.856	.037	.016	-.077	-.051	-.042	.672	-.075
28	.911	.034	.041	.063	.031	.068	.044	-.735	.017	-.014
29	.020	.025	.007	.001	.911	-.023	.033	.043	.056	-.755
30	.001	.025	.905	.016	.001	-.040	.041	.014	.788	-.025

Note. It is important to note that Clark included items which
loaded + or -.55 into a particular factor. The Modified TOSFQ
included the largest loading for each particular item (+ or -) in
the factor into which it loaded.

Table 11

Factor Structure of Clark's TOSFQ
and the Present TOSFQ

	Clark's TOSFQ					Present TOSFQ				
Factors	1	2	3	4	5	1	2	3	4	5
Items	1	3	4	5	6	3	1	2	4	6
	2	7	8	12	13	7	5	14	8	13
	9	10	11	16	22	10	9	28	11	16
	14	15	18	21	29	15	12		18	22
	19	17	23	24		17	19		23	29
	25	20	27			20	21		27	
	28	26	30			26	24		30	
							25			

For clarification purposes, factor arrangements and factor identifications of both Clark's TOSFQ and the present TOSFQ are presented here. Clark's five factors and their respective items are presented first.

Factor 1: Professional Inadequacy:

 Item 1. Trying to motivate students who do not want to learn

 Item 2. Feeling my salary is not equal to my duties and responsibilities

 Item 9. Feeling too many parents are indifferent about school problems

 Item 14. Working for an inadequate salary

Item 19. Feeling that a few difficult to discipline students take too much of my time away from other students.

Item 25. Feeling there is a lack of parental involvement in solving school discipline problems

Item 28. Feeling my job does not provide the financial security I need.

Factor 2: Teacher-Principal Professional Relationships:

Item 3. Feeling there is a lack of administrative support for teachers in my school

Item 7. Feeling my principal lacks insight into classroom problems

Item 10. Feeling my opinions are not valued by my principal

Item 15. Feeling my principal gives me too little authority to carry out the responsibilities assigned to me

Item 17. Feeling there is a lack of recognition for good teaching in my school

Item 20. Feeling I cannot tell my principal in an open way how I feel about many school related matters

Item 26. Feeling my principal is too aloof and detached from the classroom

Factor 3: Collegial Relationships:

Item 4. Working in a school where there is an atmosphere of conflict among teachers

Item 8. Feeling some teachers in my school are incompetent

Item 11. Feeling there is competition among teachers in my school rather than a team spirit of cooperation

Item 18. Feeling poor teacher/teacher relationships exist in my school

Item 23. Having a few teachers in my school who do not carry their share of the load

Item 27. Feeling that cliques exist among teachers in my school

Item 30. Feeling that poor communications exist among teachers in my school

Factor 4: Group Instruction:

Item 5. Having students in my class/classes who talk constantly

Item 12. Having to tell my students the same things over and over

Item 16. Planning and organizing learning activities for wide ability ranges

Item 21. Feeling my students do not adequately respond to my teaching

Item 24. Feeling I do not have adequate control of my students

Factor 5: Job Overload:

    Item 6. Having to do school work at home to meet what is expected of me

    Item 13. Having insufficient opportunity for rest and preparation during the school day

    Item 22. Having too little clerical help

    Item 29. Feeling I never catch up with my work

Oblique and varimax factor anaylses computed on the data collected in the present study revealed some minor discrepencies, but nothing which could be considered radically different from Clark's findings. As in Clark's study, five viable areas (factors) representing teachers' perceptions of stress emerged. The major difference was found to be in the arrangement of areas the teachers perceived to be stressful. Although the differences found are not major and basically represent some new item locations and factor arrangements, they are reported here to help the reader better understand those differences which did occur. The revised factor headings of the Modified TOSFQ and the items contained within each are the following:

Factor 1: Administrative Support:

    Item 3. Feeling there is a lack of administrative support in my school

    Item 7. Feeling my principal lacks insight into classroom problems

    Item 10. Feeling my opinions are not valued by my principal

Item 15. Feeling my principal gives me too little authority to carry out the responsibilities assigned to me

Item 17. Feeling there is a lack of recognition for good teaching in my school

Item 20. Feeling I cannot tell my principal in an open way how I feel about many school related matters

Item 26. Feeling my principal is too aloof and detached from the classroom

Factor 2: Working with Students:

Item 1. Trying to motivate students who do not want to learn

Item 5. Having students in my class/classes who talk constantly

Item 9. Feeling too many parents are indifferent about school problems

Item 12. Having to tell my students the same things over and over

Item 19. Feeling that a few difficult to discipline students take too much of my time away from the other students

Item 21. Feeling my students do not adequately respond to my teaching

Item 24. Feeling I do not have adequate control of my students

Item 25. Feeling there is a lack of parental involvement in solving discipline problems

Factor 3: Financial Security:

Item 2. Feeling my salary is not equal to my duties and responsibilities

Item 14. Working for an inadequate salary

Item 28. Feeling my job does not provide the financial security I need

Factor 4: Relationships with Teachers:

Item 4. Working in a school where there is an atmosphere of conflict among teachers

Item 8. Feeling some teachers in my school are incompetent

Item 11. Feeling there is competition among teachers in my school rather than a team spirit of cooperation

Item 18. Feeling poor teacher/teacher relationships exist in my school

Item 23. Having a few teachers in my school who do not carry their share of the load

Item 27. Feeling that cliques exist among teachers in my school

Item 30. Feeling that poor communications exist among teachers in my school

Factor 5: Task Overload:

>Item 6. Having to do school work at home to meet what is expected of me

>Item 13. Having insufficient opportunity for rest and preparation during the school day

>Item 16. Planning and organizing learning activities for wide ability ranges

>Item 22. Having too little clerical help

>Item 29. Feeling I never catch up with my work

Items which loaded in Clark's TOSFQ five factors and the items which loaded in the Modified TOSFQ's revised factors are compared in Table A of the Appendix. Table 12 illustrates the correlation findings among the five factors of the TOSFQ and the Modified TOSFQ.

Clark's factor analysis procedure revealed general support for her five factors. However, the factor analysis of the present study produced some of the rearrangement of items in factor composition. The new item composition in the factor rearrangement appeared to be more internally consistent based on conceptual considerations of the particular factors. An examination of the items in the five factors of both the TOSFQ and the modified TOSFQ should make this phenomenon clear to the reader. A decision was made to use the rearranged factors as a basis for measuring perceived stress. Results are based on scores on the revised instrument.

Table 12

Factor Correlation Comparisons of
TOSFQ and Modified TOSFQ

TOSFQ Correlations	Modified TOSFQ Correlations
<u>1</u> 1.00	1.00
<u>2</u> .18 1.00	.27 1.00
<u>3</u> .23 .24 1.00	-.31 -.26 1.00
<u>4</u> .35 .03 .26 1.00	.50 .29 -.32 1.00
<u>5</u> .45 .20 .02 .30 1.00	-.24 -.49 .43 -.27 1.00

Figure 2 provides the reader (in graph form) the means and the standard deviations computed on Factors 1-5 of the Modified TOSFQ. Because the revised instrument has a different arrangement of items for the five factors, it was not possible to compare means and standard deviations against Clark's (1980) results.

Regression Analyses of Predictor Variables

Regression analyses used eight predictors of perceived stress: Obsessive-Compulsive Ideations (OC, items 41-50); Teacher Belief Systems (TBS, items 31-40); Marital Status (MS, item 87); Sex of Principal (SOP, item 95); Years Teaching Experience (YTE, item 90); Special Education Teacher (SET, item 91); Type of School (TOS, item 92); and School Setting (SS, item 93).

75

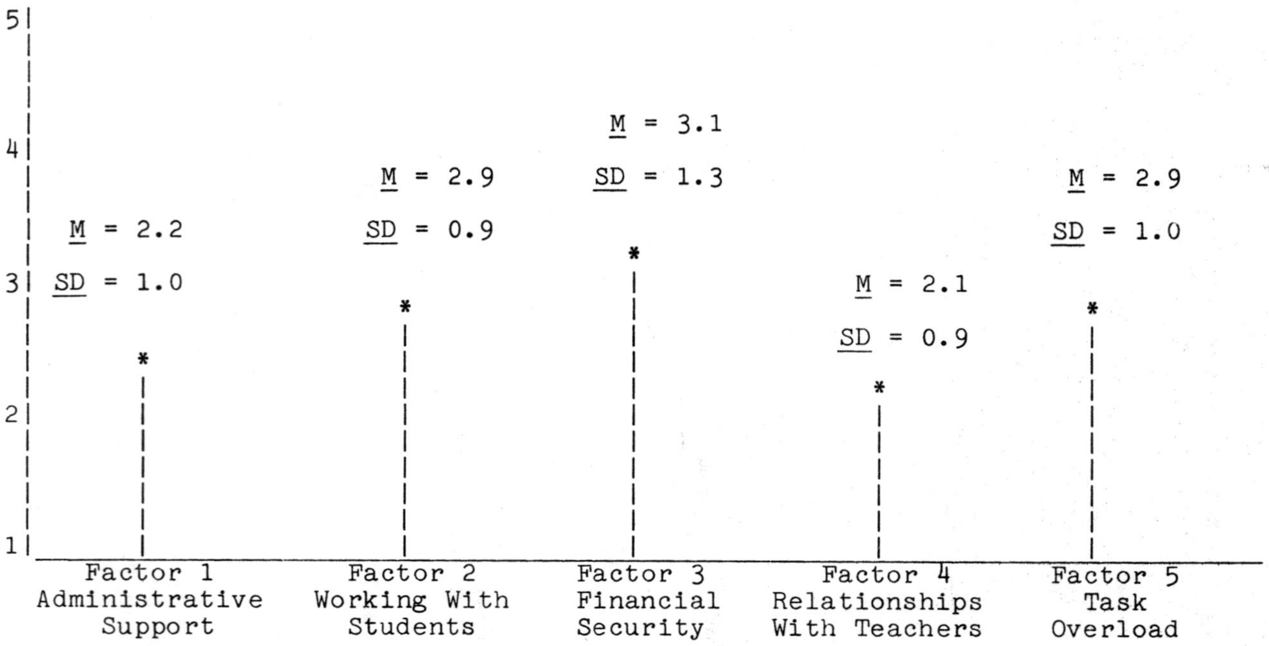

Figure 2. Means and Standard Deviations of Modified TOSFQ's Five Factors (1 = Not Stressful; 2 = Somewhat Stressful; 3 = Considerably Stressful; 4 = Decidedly Stressful; 5 = Extremely Stressful)

The eight predictors of perceived teacher stress were analyzed as independent variables for each of the five factors of the Modified TOSFQ employing multiple regression techniques. This statistical process has been explained as a "general technique through which one can analyze the relationship between a dependent or criterion variable [Factors 1-5] and a set of independent or predictor variables (Nie et al., 1975, p. 321).

Additionally, multiple regression analysis was selected because it is an appropriate technique of analyzing continuous and categorical independent variables and unequal cell frequencies.

Multiple regression analysis is superior or the only appropriate method of analysis: (1) when the independent variable is continuous, that is experimental treatments with varying degrees of the same variable: (2) when the independent variables are both continuous and categorical, as in anaylsis of covariance, or treatments by levels designs: (3) when cell frequencies in a factorial design are unequal and disproportionate: (4) when studying trends in data: linear, quadratic, and so on (Kerlinger & Pedhazur, 1973, p. 114).

Post hoc analyses were used where appropriate. For all analyses, the .05 level was established as the basis for statistical significance. Higher levels will be reported where appropriate.

Factor 1

Factor 1 of the Modified TOSFQ, Administrative Support, contained seven items (3, 7, 10, 15, 17, 20, and 26) which concern teachers' perceptions of stress as they relate to the lack of support received from administrative personnel in their schools. Items such as "Feeling there is a lack of administrative support for teachers in my school" and "Feeling my principal gives me too little authority to carry out the responsibilities assigned to me" are included in Factor 1.

Table 13 is a summary table reporting data about the eight variables which have been entered into the regression equation as they relate to Factor 1. It should be noted that the multiple regression and factor analysis treatment of the data was computer generated according to SPSS procedures. Due to missing data on one or more of the variables being measured, $\underline{N}$ = 691 was reduced to $\underline{N}$ = 660. The option, Listwise Deletion, was chosen because it "is the only way to ensure that the factor analysis is computed on the same set of cases" (Nie et al., 1975, p. 504). Years Teaching Experience, School Setting, and Sex of Principal were computed to be significant. The remaining five variables were not significant with respect to Factor 1. It is important to note, however, that the reader "should be aware that the standard $\underline{F}$ test for a partial regression coefficient gives credit to each variable only for its incremental contribution after all the other independent variables have been introduced in the equation" (Nie et al., 1975, p. 338).

Mean scores ($\overline{X}$ = 2.27, $\underline{n}$ = 221) for teachers in schools having female principals were significantly greater than mean scores ($\overline{X}$ = 2.09, $\underline{n}$ = 455) for teachers in schools having male principals, $\underline{F}$ (1, 651) = 7.277, $\underline{p}$ < .01. The results of this study indicated that teachers perceived more stress emanating from lack of administrative support in schools having female principals.

Analysis of variance and the Scheffe test were used to determine significant differences in mean scores for teachers in rural, suburban, and urban settings. Mean scores ($\overline{X}$ = 2.51, $\underline{n}$ = 74) for teachers in urban school settings were significantly greater than mean scores ($\overline{X}$ = 2.11, $\underline{n}$ = 599) for teachers in suburban school settings, $\underline{F}$ (2, 681) = 5.631, $\underline{p}$ < .005.

Table 13

Summary of Multiple Regression Analysis
Factor 1: Administrative Support

Variable	Multiple R	R2	RSQ Change	Simple R	Beta	F
TBS	.03365	.00113	.00113	.03365	.04262	1.158
OC	.03835	.00147	.00034	-.00931	-.02116	.286
YTE	.15842	.02510	.02362	-.15323	-.15207	14.274**
SS	.19370	.03752	.01242	.12842	.10776	7.734*
SOP	.21842	.04771	.01019	.10094	.10534	7.277*
TOS	.22145	.04904	.00133	-.02186	-.02887	.472
MS	.22238	.04945	.00041	.00782	.02113	.300
SET	.22334	.04988	.00043	-.01336	.02389	.295

Note. The degrees of freedom for each F ratio for each variable are 1 and 651 (Nie et al., 1975, p. 337).   *p<.01   **p<.001

Post hoc analysis of variance with respect to Years Teaching Experience (1-5, 6-10, 11-15, 16-20, and 21 or more) and its relationship to Factor 1 indicated that there were significant mean score differences between teachers with six to 10 years teaching experience ($\bar{X}$ = 2.37, $\underline{n}$ = 207) and teachers with 16-20 years teaching experience ($\bar{X}$ = 1.97, $\underline{n}$ = 109). Additionally, teachers having 6 to 10 years experience had greater mean scores than teachers having 21 or more years of experience ($\bar{X}$ = 1.87, $\underline{n}$ = 80), $\underline{F}$ (4, 680) = 4.879, $\underline{p}$ < .001. There were no significant differences between the mean scores for any other pairs of years teaching experience.

Factor 2

Factor 2 of the Modified TOSFQ, Working With Students, contained eight items (1, 5, 9, 12, 19, 21, 24, and 25) which provided data concerning teachers' perceptions of stress as they relate to their day-to-day interactions with students. Items such as "Feeling that a few difficult to discipline students take too much of my time away from other students" and "Feeling I do not have adequate control of my students" are included in this factor. Table 14 is a summary table reporting data concerning the eight independent variables which have been entered into the regression equation as they relate to Factor 2.

The variables school setting, type of school, and Special Education Teacher were significant. The remaining five variables were not. Regular classroom teachers ($\bar{X}$=3.01, $\underline{n}$=542) had significantly greater scores than special education teachers ($\bar{X}$=2.52, $\underline{n}$=130). Table 14 reports the significant findings. The findings for Type of School yielded significant differences between teachers' average scores (see Table 15) in special education centers and teachers' average scores in the four remaining types of schools. Mean scores for teachers housed in middle or junior high school were significantly greater than the mean scores for teachers found in senior high schools, ($\underline{F}$=4,683)=18.31, $\underline{p}$ < .001.

Table 14

Summary of Multiple Regression Analysis
Factor 2: Working With Students

Variable	Multiple R	R2	RSQ Change	Simple R	Beta	F
TBS	.05648	.00319	.00319	-.05648	-.03723	.928
OC	.05891	.00347	.00028	-.03047	-.01918	.246
SET	.23584	.05562	.05215	.22837	.16109	14.099*
SS	.27007	.07294	.01732	.14872	.12531	11.001*
TOS	.29642	.08787	.01493	-.20884	-.13812	11.353*
SOP	.30376	.09227	.00440	-.10120	-.06589	2.992
YTE	.30628	.09381	.00154	-.00448	-.04097	1.106
MS	F or Tolerance Level Insufficient for Further Computation					

Note. The degrees of freedom for each F ratio for each variable are 1 and 651 (Nie et al., 1975, p. 337).
*$p < .001$.

Table 15

Means and Numbers for Types of Schools
on Factor 2: Working With Students

Types of Schools	Means	Number of Teachers
Elementary (K-6)	2.91	235
Middle (7-8)/Junior (7-9)	3.12	243
High School (9-12)	3.08	69
Senior High School (10-12)	2.72	78
Special Education Center	2.18	63

Results of the post hoc tests revealed significant differences in mean scores of teachers in rural ($\bar{X}$ = 2.48, n = 11), suburban ($\bar{X}$ = 2.89, n = 599), and urban ($\bar{X}$ = 3.18, n = 74) school settings. Mean scores for teachers in urban school settings were significantly greater than the mean scores for teachers in both rural and suburban school settings, F (2, 681) = 5.301, p < .005. The mean scores for teachers in rural and suburban school settings were not significantly different.

Factor 3

Factor 3 of the Modified TOSFQ, Financial Security, contained three items (2, 14, and 28). All three are concerned with teachers' perceptions of stress as they relate to salary and financial concerns, for example, "Feeling my job does not provide the financial security I need." Table 16 is a summary of the multiple regression analysis of the eight variables and their relationship to Factor 3.

Table 16

Summary of Multiple Regression Analysis
Factor 3: Financial Security

Variable	Multiple R	R2	RSQ Change	Simple R	Beta	F
TBS	.03888	.00151	.00151	-.03888	-.02802	.498
OC	.04153	.00172	.00021	-.02393	-.00810	.042
YTE	.17027	.02899	.02727	-.16663	-.16202	16.119*
MS	.18418	.03392	.00493	-.08890	-.06766	3.058
SOP	.19587	.03836	.00444	-.07096	-.05918	2.285
SS	.20635	.04258	.00422	.08221	.06006	2.390
SET	.21124	.04462	.00204	.02411	.03868	.769
TOS	.21219	.04502	.00040	-.02991	-.02203	.273

Note. The degrees of freedom for each F ratio for each variable are 1 and 651 (Nie et al., 1975, p. 337). *p < .001

83

Years Teaching Experience was the only variable that was significant on Factor 3. The variable was categorized in five year intervals. Results of the post hoc tests revealed that less experienced teachers perceived more stress than did teachers with more experience. Teachers with 6-10 years of teaching experience perceived more stress ($\overline{X} = 3.32$, $\underline{n} = 105$) than either teachers with 16-20 years of teaching experience ($\overline{X} = 2.86$, $\underline{n} = 105$) or teachers with 21 or more years of teaching experience ($\overline{X} = 2.60$, $\underline{n} = 80$). Teachers with 1-5 years of teaching experience (X = 3.20, $\underline{n} = 105$) perceived more stress than did teachers with 21 or more years of experience, $\underline{F}(4, 680) = 5.860$, $\underline{p} < .001$.

Factor 4

Factor 4 of the Modified TOSFQ, Relationships With Teachers, contained seven items (4, 8, 11, 18, 23, 27, and 30) which concern teachers' perceptions of stress as they relate to daily interactions with colleagues. Items such as "Feeling that cliques exist among teachers in my school" and "Feeling that poor communications exist among teachers in my school" are included. Table 17 summarizes the regression analysis of the variables as they relate to Factor 4.

Three of the eight variables were significant for this factor. School Setting, Sex of Principal and Obsessive-Compulsive Ideations were significant beyond .005. Differences in mean scores indicated that teachers located in urban school settings ($\overline{X} = 2.39$, $\underline{n} = 74$) perceived more stress than did teachers in suburban school settings ($\overline{X} = 2.11$, $\underline{n} = 599$), $\underline{F}(2, 681) = 3.713$, $\underline{p} < .025$. Other comparisons of pairs proved not to be significant.

The mean score for teachers in schools having female principals was 2.25 ($\underline{n} = 221$). The mean score for teachers in schools having male principals was 2.09 ($\underline{n} = 455$). Multiple regression analysis indicated that teachers perceived more stress emanating from lack of administrative support in schools having female principals, $F(1, 651) = 8.719$, $p < .005$.

Obsessive-Compulsive Ideations, the measure of perfectionistic attitude, was also significant with respect to Factor 4. This multi-item psychological variable ($\bar{X} = 32.30$, $SD = 5.44$, $n = 660$) proved to have a significant relationship beyond the .005 level.

Factor 5

Factor 5 of the Modified TOSFQ, Task Overload, contained five items (6, 13, 16, 22, and 29) which relate to teachers' perceptions of stress as they carry out the activities of the teaching profession. Items such as "Having to do school work at home to meet what is expected of me" and "Feeling I never catch up with my work" are included in this factor. Table 18 reports the regression findings of the eight variables as they relate to Factor 5.

Mean scores for teachers in special education centers were significantly lower than mean scores of teachers in each of the other four types of schools, $F(4, 683) = 7.639$, $p < .001$. Mean scores are reported in Table 19.

Table 17

Summary of Multiple Regression Analysis
Factor 4: Relationships With Teachers

Variable	Multiple R	R2	RSQ Change	Simple R	Beta	F
OC	.09179	.00842	.00842	-.09179	-.11722	8.783*
TBS	.11609	.01348	.00505	.04563	.07685	3.773
SS	.17217	.02964	.01616	.12561	.11926	9.494*
SOP	.20771	.04314	.01350	.11128	.11518	8.719*
YTE	.22115	.04891	.00576	-.09338	-.07168	3.178
TOS	.22456	.05043	.00152	-.02710	-.04500	1.149
MS	.22748	.05175	.00132	-.03891	-.03719	.931
SET	.22812	.05204	.00029	-.03133	-.01964	.200

Note. The degrees of freedom for each F ratio for each variable are 1 and 651 (Nie et al., 1975, p. 337).
*$p < .005$

Table 18

Summary of Multiple Regression Analysis
Factor 5: Task Overload

Variable	Multiple R	R2	RSQ Change	Simple R	Beta	F
OC	.05909	.00349	.00349	-.05909	-.06637	2.814
TBS	.06017	.00362	.00013	-.00391	-.02503	.399
TOS	.19059	.03633	.03271	-.17881	-.15581	13.766*
SS	.20496	.04201	.00568	.08249	.06633	2.927
SET	.21169	.04481	.00281	.12571	.06753	2.444
MS	.21418	.04587	.00106	.02836	.03711	.924
YTE	.21688	.04714	.00116	-.00954	-.03593	.797
SOP	F or Tolerance Level Insufficient for Further Computation					

Note. The degrees of freedom for each F ratio for each variable are 1 and 651 (Nie et al., 1975, p. 337).
*p<.001

Table 19

Means and Numbers for Types of Schools
on Factor 5: Task Overload

Types of Schools	Means	Number of Teachers
Elementary (K-6)	3.06	235
Middle (7-8)/Junior (7-9)	2.90	243
High School (9-12)	2.90	69
Senior High School (10-12)	2.86	78
Special Education Center	2.29	63

Summary of Results

With respect to each of the five identified occupational stress factors, the following variables were found to be significant.

Factor 1: Administrative Support

1. Years Teaching Experience, Variable 90
2. School Setting, Variable 93
3. Sex of Principal, Variable 95

Factor 2: Working With Students

1. Special Education Teacher (versus regular classroom teacher), Variable 91
2. Type of School, Variable 92
3. School Setting, Variable 93

Factor 3: Financial Security

  1. Years Teaching Experience, Variable 90

Factor 4: Relationships With Teachers

  1. School Setting, Variable 93
  2. Sex of Principal, Variable 95
  3. Obsessive-Compulsive Ideations, Variables 41-50

Factor 5: Task Overload

  1. Type of School, Variable 92

The aforementioned data and levels of significance are reported in Table 20.

Based on the statistical results reported in this chapter, the following null hypotheses on a factor by factor consideration were rejected or not rejected at the .05 level of significance (see Table 21).

H_1: There is no significant difference in mean scores between special education and other classroom teachers on each of the occupational stress factors. (Reject)

H_2: There is no significant difference between mean scores of teachers who teach in rural, urban, or suburban school settings with respect to each of the occupational stress factors. (Reject)

H_3: There is no significant difference between mean scores of teachers who teach in elementary, middle/junior high, high, senior high, and special education schools (centers) with respect to each of the occupational stress factors. (Reject)

Table 20

Significance Levels of the Eight Independent Variables Across the Five Factors of the Modified TOSFQ

Variable	Factor 1 Administrative Support	Factor 2 Working With Students	Factor 3 Financial Security	Factor 4 Relationships With Teachers	Factor 5 Task Overload
SET	NS	.001	NS	NS	NS
SS	.01	.001	NS	.005	NS
TOS	NS	.001	NS	NS	.001
SOP	.01	NS	NS	.005	NS
MS	NS	NS	NS	NS	NS
YTE	.001	NS	.001	NS	NS
TBS	NS	NS	NS	NS	NS
OC	NS	NS	NS	.005	NS

Note. NS represents not significant.

H_4: There is no significant difference between mean scores of teachers who teach in schools having male principals and teachers who teach in schools having female principal with respect to each of the occupational stress factors. (Reject)

H_5: There is no significant difference between mean scores of single, married, divorced, or widowed teachers with respect to each of the occupational stress factors. (Accept)

H_6: There is no significant difference between mean scores of teachers who have 1-5, 6-10, 11-15, 16-20, or more than 21 years teaching experience with respect to each occupational stress factor. (Reject)

H_7: There is no significant relationship between mean scores of teachers' belief systems and each occupational stress factor. (Accept)

H_8: There is no significant relationship between mean scores of teachers' obsessive-compulsive ideations and each occupational stress factor. (Reject)

Perusal of Table 21 delineated that six hypotheses were rejected on at least one of the five factors. Hypothesis$_2$ was most frequently rejected. This hypothesis concerned teachers in different school settings. Generally, urban teachers perceived more stress than either rural or suburban teachers. Hypotheses $_3$, $_4$, and $_6$ were rejected on two factors each. These hypotheses concerned school types, sex of principal, and years of teaching experience respectively. Hypothesis$_8$ was rejected on only one factor. This hypothesis concerned teachers' obsessive-compulsive ideations. The data failed to reject Hypotheses$_5$ and $_7$ on any of the five factors. These hypotheses concerned teachers' marital status and belief systems respectively.

Table 21

Decision to Reject the Eight Hypotheses
Across the Five Factors of the Modified TOSFQ

Hyp.	Factor 1 Administrative Support	Factor 2 Working With Students	Factor 3 Financial Security	Factor 4 Relationships With Teachers	Factor 5 Task Overload
H_1		Reject			
H_2	Reject	Reject		Reject	
H_3		Reject			Reject
H_4	Reject			Reject	
H_5					
H_6	Reject		Reject		
H_7					
H_8				Reject	

V. DISCUSSION

This chapter presents a summary of the study, the conclusions which can be drawn from the data analyses, and recommendations for further research and inquiry. The study's primary purpose was to investigate the differences between special education and other classroom teachers' perceptions of occupational stress factors. Secondary purposes of the investigation were to delineate differences that existed on the demographic and psychological variables with respect to teacher stress. Teachers' Belief Systems and Obsessive-Compulsive Ideation measured how teachers thought about themselves and their students. Marital Status, Years Teaching Experience, Sex of Principal, School Setting, and Type of School measured the demographic variables. The TOSFQ (Clark, 1980) was the instrument selected and modified to collect the data.

Factor Structure

Similar to the study conducted by Clark (1980), factor analysis produced five factors on the 30-item instrument. (The factors, although similar to Clark's findings, were not identical.) These five factors were relabeled Administrative Support, Working with Students, Financial Security, Relationships with Teachers, and Task Overload.

The findings of the present study are summarized by comparing the similarities and differences with the studies conducted by Clark (1980) and Cichon and Koff (1978), as well as other studies reported in the literature. Table 22 illustrates the areas or factors of teachers' perceptions of occupational stress factors as identified by Cichon and Koff, Clark, and the present study.

Table 22

A Comparison of Stress Factors Among Three Studies

Stress Area Rank	Cichon and Koff (1978)	Clark (1980)	Present Study
1	Priority Concerns (Violence and Student Discipline)	Professional Inadequacy (Financial and Pedagogical Concerns)	Administrative Support (Administrative Concerns)
2	Management Tension (Administrative or "Imposed" Stress)	Principal/Teacher Professional Relationships (Administrative Concerns)	Working with Students (Student Discipline and Teaching Concerns)
3	Doing a Good Job (Professionalism)	Collegial Relationships (Relationships with other Teachers)	Financial Security (Salary-Related Concerns)
4	Pedagogical Functions (Actual Teaching Functions)	Group Instruction (Teaching and Student Discipline Concerns)	Relationships with Teachers (Collegial Relationship Concerns)
5		Job Overload (Work Load Concerns)	Task Overload (Work Load Concerns)

The three studies included in Table 22 were conducted in different locations. Cichon and Koff conducted their study in the Chicago inner-city school system. Clark's study was conducted in Alabama and Georgia. Though not addressed by Clark, it can be assumed that her study involved more teachers from rural areas than the study conducted by Cichon and Koff. The present study was conducted in an area overwhelmingly identified as suburban by the teachers who participated in it. The different settings may account for the different responses. Additionally, one should keep in mind when interpreting these data that:

> There are no a priori criteria for determining stressful versus nonstressful events. In fact, it is assumed that even those events of lowest rank induce some degree of stress, however mild. The data, therefore, do not indicate how well teachers are adapting to the stress they report, nor do the data provide information about how well teachers are performing. What the data do show is the relative degree of stress of events [factors in the Clark and present study]; the meaning of the weights assigned to events is, obviously, open to interpretation (Cichon & Koff, 1978, p. 7).

Factor 1, Administrative Support, was found to be the most stress producing. It contributed 54.2% of the total variance in the factor analysis. Although this is in disagreement with Cichon and Koff's (1978) findings, the literature is replete with data supporting both--discipline problems in schools (including violence) and administrative concerns--as leading producers of stress. The teachers included in the present study indicated that the lack of administrative support, absence of insight on part of their principals, little communication between them and their principals, and insufficient principal recognition for good teaching were perceived as stressful. These teachers felt that their principals did not value their opinions, restricted teachers' authority to carry out their assigned responsibilities, and remained too aloof and detached from the classroom. Summarizing, it can be stated that the teachers indicated that the gap between the school administrators (principals) and the teaching staffs has to be diminished in order for teachers to perceive their work environment as less stressful. Apparently there exists a significant lack of communication between teachers and principals in this school system.

Factor 2, Working with Students, appears to be conceptually consistent with Cichon and Koff's first cluster, Priority Concerns, with the exceptions of items 9 and 25, which are concerned with teacher-parent interactions. These two items (9 and 25) were included in Clark's Factor 1; however, other items in her Factor 1 include a variety of teaching concerns (e.g., motivation, salary, discipline). Factor 2 contributed 18.3% of the variance in the factor analysis of the present study. The items included in this factor (1, 5, 9, 12, 19, 21, 24, and 25) add further support to the fact that the ways teachers feel about themselves and their students are significant in determining perceived occupational stress factors in the teaching profession. Teachers' feelings of inadequacy--not being able to motivate reluctant learners, not being able to control their class/classes, not being able to effectively involve parents in solving discipline problems--pervade this perceived area of teacher stress.

Factor 3, Financial Security, included three items (2, 14, and 28) concerned with salary issues. There is no comparable area in the Cichon and Koff study, and these items fell into Clark's "catch-all" Factor 1. Factor 3 contributed 11.4% of the variance in the factor analysis of the present study. The responses to the items clearly indicate that teachers feel that their salaries are inadequate, are not commensurate with their responsibilities, and do not provide them financial security. Given the context of contemporary society with its inflationary features, the impact of these concerns can be appreciated.

Factor 4, Relationships with Teachers, is identical to Factor 3, Collegial Relationships, in Clark's (1980) study. Since the items in Factor 4 of the present study proved to be identical to those in Clark's third factor, it seemed prudent to compare mean scores from both studies. Interpolating information provided by Clark (1980, p. 97), the mean score for her sample on Factor 3 was 2.84. The mean score on Factor 4 of the present study was 2.77 (rounded off to 2.8 in Figure 2). Teachers in both studies resoponded to the items in like fashion. It would appear that teachers interacting with teachers produces stress. Since the items in these two factors are concerned only with how teachers interact with fellow teachers, they are conceptually clear.

Factor 4 contributed 10.3% of the variance in the present study. In both the Clark and current studies it is a perceived stress factor; however, the teachers who participated in the present study had responses that indicated by rank that collegial relationships were not as stressful to them as to those teachers in the study conducted by Clark.

Factor 5, Task Overload, in the present study and Factor 5, Job Overload, in Clark's (1980) study had identical items and also can be considered conceptually clear since the items which comprise these two factors were concerned with the amount of work teachers are expected to accomplish. Interpolating data provided by Clark (1980, p. 105), the mean score for her sample on the items which comprise Factor 5 was 3.26. For the present study it was 2.62 (rounded off to 2.6 in Figure 2). Thus these concerns--taking school work home, insufficient time for rest and preparation during school hours, lack of clerical help, and feeling unable to catch up with their work--proved to be considerably more stress producing for teachers in Clark's study than they were for teachers included in the present study.

It may be that teachers in the current study had more paraprofessional help, preparation periods, and breaks than the Georgia and Alabama teachers.

Table 23 summarizes the eigenvalues and percentage of variance of the five factors analyzed in the present study. Since item placement and factor arrangement were not consistent between Clark's (1980) TOSFQ and the Modified TOSFQ, a factor by factor comparision was not possible.

Table 23

Eigenvalues and Percentage of Variance
of Present Study's Five Factors

Factor	Eigenvalue	Percentage of Variance	Cumulative Percentage
1	8.69998	54.2	54.2
2	2.93382	18.3	72.5
3	1.83508	11.4	83.9
4	1.65649	10.3	94.2
5	0.93684	5.8	100.0

Differences in factor rankings between Clark's (1980) study and the present study may be accounted for by the fact that Clark's investigation included a randomly selected group of Alabama teachers whose salaries are substantially less than the salaries of those who participated in the current study. Furthermore, the mood of the Alabama State Legislature when Clark was conducting her research is noteworthy. Teachers' salary increases were an intensely debated issue, and conditions were not promising for a teachers' salary increase to be ratified.

> "Salary questions were considered major issues by Alabama teachers and were possibly perceived as being greater contributors to job-induced stress during the time the questionnaire was being responded to than if the salary question had not been in the legislature" (Clark, 1980, p. 82).

No salary or finance related item appeared in Factor 1 of the Modified TOSFQ. These and the other discrepancies already mentioned led this researcher to believe that the factor items loaded with more conceptual clarity on the Modified TOSFQ (see Appendix C, Table 24).

Predictor Variables

"Regardless of sex, race, age, type of school, etc., teachers share common perceptions concerning stress associated with teaching" (Cichon & Koff, 1978, p. 7). The findings of this study contradict this claim. Teachers in urban, suburban, and rural school settings did not share the same perceptions on the Modified TOSFQ. Urban teachers perceived more stress on Factor 1, administrative Support, Factor 2, Working With Students, and Factor 4, Relationships With Teachers. Data collected in this study indicate that teaching in urban school settings is more stressful than teaching in either suburban or rural settings. On the other hand, the results of this study lend support to Collins' (1980) claim that there are prominent environmental sources of stress. Additionally, the results help answer the question raised by Cichon and Koff (1978) of whether urban school settings are more stressful than suburban and/or rural school settings. The reader is reminded that the Cichon and Koff study was conducted in an urban school system.

Explanations of why urban teachers perceived more stress on Factor 1, Administrative Support, are presented with a degree of caution. Since the assignment of administrative personnel where this study occurred is made on a per pupil basis and since teaching in urban schools may be more demanding, teachers in these schools perceived a lack of administrative support.

Similarly, explanations for differences on Factor 4, Relationships With Teachers, with regard to school settings, focus on the inherent environmental concerns associated with urban schools. It may be that there is a norm within teachers that values teaching in rural and suburban settings rather than urban school settings. Thus it may be that teachers found in urban school settings possess characteristics that mitigate against facilitative interaction with their peers. This finding agrees with the claim made by Cichon and Koff (1978) that where one teaches is an "imposed" source of stress, since the teacher has little or no control over his/her school assignment.

Less experienced teachers with respect to Factor 1, Administrative Support, and Factor 3, Financial Security, perceived more stress than did more experienced teachers. This finding contradicts the findings of Clark (1980). Interpretation of the data collected in her study revealed that there was no difference in teachers' perceptions of job induced stress. It may be that less experienced teachers did not necessarily perceive inadequacies any differently from the more experienced teachers. Interpretation of the data collected in the present study indicated that less experienced teachers perceived concerns associated with the lack of administrative support to be more stress producing than veteran teachers did. It is likely that veteran teachers enjoy a greater feeling of job security, and are not as predisposed to to the need for support from school administrators. With respect to Financial Security, teachers in the 6-10 years of teaching experience interval are more likely to bear the demands of our inflationary society. It can be safely assumed that the majority of teachers found in the aforementioned interval are at that point in their lives when their incomes do not adequately compensate for these societal demands.

Sex of Principal proved to be an influential variable on Factors 1 and 4. Teachers in schools having female principals perceived more stress on both these factors. With respect to sex of principal and administrative support, this finding may be an artifact of the sexual composition of the responding teachers in this sample. Women comprised 68.7% of the respondents.

Similar conclusions can be drawn about sex of principal and Factor 4, Relationships With Teachers. However, any definite conclusions must be drawn with caution.

For the variable, Type of School, it was found to significantly influence perceptions of stress on Factors 2 and 5. These factors concern working with students and task overload respectively. Teachers in special education centers perceived less stress than did teachers in other school types. To some degree, this finding contradicts the Cichon and Koff (1978) claim that the type of school has little influence on stress. Also, Clark's assertion that there are no significant differences in teacher stress according to school setting may not hold up across larger samples. In this study, teachers in middle/junior high schools perceived more stress than did senior high school teachers. It must be noted that Clark's sample did not include special education centers, and with the exception of the middle/junior high difference, there was consistency in the responses of teachers in the different school types in this study.

For the variable, Special Education Teacher, it was found that these teachers perceive less stress on Factor 2, Working With Students. This apparently contradicts the Weiskopf (1980) claim that "special educators in particular are burning out on the job" (p. 18). Related to this dimension is the finding that teachers in special education centers perceived less stress than other teachers on Factor 5, Task Overload. It may be due to special considerations for special education centers, for example, lower student/teacher ratios, the availability of more paraprofessionals, and the recent influx of monies from state and federal agencies. This also may hold true for special education teachers in comprehensive school types, for they have access to equipment, materials, and paraprofessionals not normally accorded regular classroom teachers.

Obsessive-Compulsive Ideations was significantly related to teacher stress on Factor 4, Relationships With Teachers. This lends partial support to Burchfield's (1979) position that stress is largely a psychological process. Further credence is given to the works of Bloch (1977) and Styles and Cavanagh (1977). Bloch has described teachers as being "obsessional, passive, idealistic, dedicated persons" (1977, p. 62). Styles and Cavanagh have also written much concerning the generation of stress from within the teacher.

Specifically, the Obsessive-Compulsive Ideations section of the Modified TOSFQ was designed to measure the degree of perfectionistic attitude held by an individual (Burns, 1980). Examples of some items included in this section are the following: "People will think less of me if I make a mistake" and "Failing at something important means I'm less of a person." Individuals who score high on this scale are thought to be compulsive worriers. Consequently, teachers who are "worriers" will probably anticipate the painful consequences of stressful events even before they occur. Burchfield (1979) believes that these anticipations produce physiological changes in an individual as though they were the actual stressors.

The findings in the present study corroborated the data collected by a 1980 NEA survey of 1,783 randomly selected teachers across the nation. According to the NEA study, 35% of the nation's teachers are "dissatisfied" with their current teaching positions, and 9% are "very dissatisfied." When asked what career they would choose if they could begin again, 41% reported they would not or probably would not become teachers if they had the opportunity to choose their careers over. The NEA study further reported that: "Exactly 9% will leave teaching as soon as they can, with another 20% undecided. Only 43% say they will continue until retirement" (NEA Survey, 1980, p. 49). The findings of the current study on job satisfaction are consistent with the NEA study. NEA reported that teachers in larger school systems (more than 25,000 students) are more dissatisfied than those in smaller systems. As previously mentioned, the present study was undertaken in a system with more than 121,000 students, and 51.2% of the teachers in this study stated they would not become teachers if given the opportunity to choose their careers over. This supports NEA's figure that 41% of the teachers across the country "would not" or "probably would not" become teachers again. It should be remembered that the national study conducted by NEA included many systems with smaller student enrollments than the enrollment of the public school system where the present study's data were collected. The results of this investigation indicated that a majority of teachers are not happy with their profession. Although it is difficult to determine a specific cause-effect relationship, it is not unreasonable to assume that dissatisfaction would have an adverse effect on performance.

Implications for Future Research

Based on the findings of this study, the following suggestions are made with the hope that stress in the teaching profession may be better understood.

1. More research must be initiated to better understand the psychological composite of teachers which makes them predisposed to stress. Specifically, teacher ideations and beliefs must be further investigated to discover "across the board" commonalities.

2. More research should be conducted on the validity and reliability of the Modified TOSFQ. For example, investigations should be conducted in various geographical areas of the country or on a national level.

3. More investigations should be initiated to help teachers avoid the stress-burnout process. Much can be said for: "An ounce of prevention is worth a pound of cure."

4. More study is needed to identify other predictors of perceived stress. A better understanding of the psychological and environmental predictors of stress in the teaching profession can lead to future research aimed at more effective ways teachers can cope with stress.

5. Effective research is mandated by the results of this study to eliminate the gap which exists between school administrators and teachers, the perceived leading cause of teacher stress.

6. Research should be continued with the aim of better understanding the structure of the public school bureaucracy as a possible stressor of teachers (especially in those systems where teachers are viewed as subordinates). Such research would identify and elucidate those social and political conditions which exist in hierarchical atmospheres and spawn anxiety, tension, and stress.

7. Research should be undertaken with the aim of improving our teacher education programs. That teachers feel ineffective teaching reluctant learners, resolving discipline problems, and generally working with youngsters illustrates the urgency of this much needed research.

8. Research is needed to determine what effects teacher stress has on pupils. For example, it would be important to find out if highly stressed individuals are less effective teachers. Similarly, it would be important to ascertain if classes taught by highly stressed teachers differ from other classes. Certain differences may be hypothesized. It may be that highly stressed teachers have more discipline problems, classroom conflicts, and student absences than less stressed teachers.

Teachers, like others, need respect, recognition, and positive interaction with school administrators, colleagues, and students. They have to satisfy their lower level needs of safety and security in order to pursue their higher order need for self-actualization. Teaching in American public schools is stressful, as the results of this and other studies have indicated. The problem is well documented and the time has arrived for solutions to be realized.

REFERENCES

Alley, R. Stress and the professional educator. *Action in Teacher Education*, Fall 1980, 2 (4), 1-8.

Alschuler, A. S. Causes, consequences, and cures: A summary. In A. S. Alschuler (Ed.), *Teacher Burnout*. Washington, D.C.: National Education Association, 1980.

Anderson, B. Five quick tips to help principals reduce teacher stress. *The Executive Educator*, July 1980, p. 20.

Anderson, B. How to make sure teachers can't blame you for stress. *The Executive Educator*, July 1980, pp. 18-20; 39.

Anderson, J. G. *Bureaucy in education*. Baltimore: The Johns Hopkins Press, 1968.

Ary, D., Jacobs, L. C., & Razavieh, A. *Introduction to research in education*. New York: Holt, Rinehart, and Winston, Inc., 1972.

Ban, J. R. Teacher stress: An emerging priority in teacher education. *The Professional Educator*, Fall 1980, 3 (2), 1-5.

Bardo, P. The pain of teacher burnout. *Phi Delta Kappan*, December 1979, 61, 252-254.

Bartley, S. H. What do you mean tired? *Today's Education*, March-April 1975, pp. 54-55.

Baugh, D. S. Perceived stress among school administrative personnel (Doctoral dissertation, Ball State University, 1976). *Dissertation Abstracts International*, 1977, 37, 6264A-6265A. (University Micro-films No. 77-8652,158)

Bensky, J. M., Shaw, S. F., Gouse, A. S., Bates, H., Dixon, B., & Beane, W. E. Public Law 94-142 and stress: A problem for educators. *Exceptional Children*, September 1980, 47, 24-29.

Benson, H. *The relaxation response*. New York: William Morrow and Company, Inc., 1975.

Bentz, W. K., Hollister, S. G., & Edgerton, J. W. An assessment of the mental health of teachers: A comparative analysis. *Psychology in the Schools*, 1971, 8, 72-76.

Berger, M. *Statement regarding occupational stress among teachers*. Paper presented before the U.S. House of Representatives Sub-Committee on Elementary, Secondary, and Vocational Education, Washington, D.C., February 6, 1980.

Biersner, R. J., Bunde, G. R., Doucette, R. E., & Culwell, C. W. Counselor evaluation inventory: Replication of factor structure on a military sample. *Measurement and Evaluation in Guidance*, January 1981, 13, 223-227.

Bloch, A. M. Combat neurosis in inner city schools. *The American Journal of Psychiatry*, October 1978, 135, 1189-1192.

Bloch, A. M. The battered teacher. *Today's Education*, March-April 1977, 66, 58-62.

Broder, F. Stress and how to deal with it. *Georgia Educator*, Fall 1979, pp. 20-21.

Brown, B. B. *New mind, new body*. New York: Harper and Row, 1974.

Brown, B. B. *Stress and the art of biofeedback*. New York: Harper and Row, 1977.

Bry, A. *Getting better*. New York: Rawson, Wade Publishers, Inc., 1978.

Burchfield, S. R. The stress response: A new perspective. *Psychosomatic Medicine*, December 1979, *41*, 661-672.

Burns, D. D. The perfectionist's script for self-defeat. *Psychology Today*, November 1980, pp. 34; 37-38; 41-42; 44; 46; 50; 52.

Calhoun, G. L. Hospitals are high-stress employers. *Hospitals*, June 16, 1980, *54*, 173-176.

Cardinell, C. F. Teacher burnout: An analysis. *Action in Teacher Education*, Fall 1980, *2* (4), 9-15.

Cherry, L. The man who first named stress. *Psychology Today*, March 1978, p. 64.

Cichon, D. J., & Koff, R. H. *The teaching events stress inventory*. Paper presented to American Educational Research Association, Toronto, March 1978.

Clark, E. H. *An analysis of occupational stress factors as perceived by public school teachers*. Unpublished doctoral dissertation, Auburn University, 1980.

Coates, T. J., & Thoresen, C. E. Teacher anxiety: A review with recommendations. *Review of Educational Research*, Spring 1976, *46*, 159-184.

Cobb, S. Role responsibility: The differentiation of a concept. *Occupational Mental Health*, 1973, *3*, 10-14.

Cochrane, R., & Robertson, A. The life events inventory: A measure of the relative severity of psycho-social stressors. *Journal of Psychosomatic Research*, 1973, *17*, 135-139.

Collins, D. Some tips for coping. *Maryland State Teachers Association Action Line*, January 14, 1981, *14*, 2.

Collins, D. Stress and your personality. *Maryland State Teachers Association Action Line*, November 19, 1980, 14, 2.

Cooper, C. L., & Marshall, J. Occupational sources of stress: A review of the literature relating to coronary heart disease and mental ill health. *Journal of Occupational Psychology*, 1976, 49, 11-28.

Corwin, R. G. Militant professionalism: *A study of organizational conflict in high schools.* New York: Appleton-Century-Crofts, 1970.

Cox, T. *Stress.* Baltimore: University Park Press, 1978.

Dale, R. L. Administrators, stress, and coronary heart disease (Doctoral dissertation, Ball State University, 1976). *Dissetation Abstracts International*, 1977, 37, 6169A-6170A. (University Microfilms No. 77-8654, 139)

D'Alonzo, B. J., & Wiseman, D. E. Actual and desired role of the high school learning disability resource teacher. *Journal of Learning Dissabilities*, June/July 1978, 2, 63-70.

Dixon, B., Shaw, S., & Bensky, J. Administrator's role in fostering the mental health of special services personnel. *Exceptional Children*, September 1980, 47, 30-36.

Dollar, B. L. The effects of desensitization and behavioral skills training on situational teaching anxiety (Doctoral dissertation, University of Texas). *Dissertation Abstracts International*, 1972, 32, 7189A. (University Microfilms No. 72-15743)

Doyal, G. T., & Forsyth, R. A. The relationship between teacher and student anxiety levels. *Psychology in the Schools*, 1973, 10, 231-233.

Freudenberger, H. J. Burnout: Occupational hazard of the child care worker. *Child Care Quarterly*, Summer 1977, *6*, 90-99.

Fuller, F. F. Concerns of teachers: A developmental conceptualization. *American Educational Research Journal*, March 1969, *6*, 207-226.

Good vs. bad stress. *G. E. Monogram*, September-October 1978, pp. 38-39.

Goodall, R., & Brown, L. Understanding teacher stress. *Action in Education*, Fall 1980, *2* (4), 17-22.

Green, E., & Green, A. *Beyond biofeedback*. San Francisco: Delacorte Press, 1977.

Hanson, E. M. *Educational administration and organizational behavior*. Boston: Allyn and Bacon, Inc., 1979.

Harlin, V. K., & Jerrick, S. J. Is teaching hazardous to your health? *Instructor*, September 1976, *86*, 55-58; 212-214.

Help! Teacher can't teach! *Time*, June 16, 1980, pp. 54-63.

Hendrickson, B. Is exhausted an apt description of your present state of mind? You may be suffering from teacher burnout. But don't despair: You're not alone, and there is a cure. *Learning*, January 1979, pp. 37-38.

Hendricks, C. G., Thoresen, C. E., & Coates, T. J. *Self-managing stress and tension*. Paper presented at the Annual Meeting of the American Educational Research Association, Washington, D.C., March 30 to April 3, 1975. (Eric Document Reproduction Service No. ED 120 610)

Hendrickson, B. Teachers combat burnout. *Learning*, January 1979, p. 38.

Hicks, F. P. *The mental health of teachers*. New York: Cullman and Ghertnes, 1933.

Hinkle, L. E. The concept of stress in the biological and social sciences. *International Journal of Psychiatry in Medicine*, 1974, *5*, 335-357.

House approves program for stressed teachers. *Chicago Union Teacher*, March 1978, p. 4.

Humphrey, J. H., & Humphrey, J. N. Coping with stress through classroom isometrics. *Action in Teacher Education*, Fall 1980, *2* (4), 41-45.

Hunter, M. *Counter irritants to teaching*. Unpublished paper presented the annual meeting of the American Association of School Administrators, Las Vegas, Nevada, February 1977.

Instructor survey reveals stress, weight top concerns of teachers nation-wide. *Instructor*, February 1977, *86*, 12.

Kahn, R. L. Conflict, ambiguity and overload: Three elements in job stress. *Occupational Mental Health*, 1973, *3*, 2-9.

Kahn, R. L., & Quinn, R. P. Role stress. In McLean (ed.), *Mental Health and Work Organization*, Chicago: Rand McNally, 1970.

Kerlinger, F. N., & Pedhazur, E. J. *Multiple regression in behavioral research*. New York: Holt, Rinehart and Winston, Inc., 1973.

Koon, J. R. Effects of expectancy, anxiety, and task difficulty on teacher behavior (Doctoral dissertation, Syracuse University). *Dissertation Abstracts International*, 1971, *32*, 821A. (University Microfilms No. 71-18492)

Kossack, S. W., & Woods, S. L. Teacher burnout: Diagnosis, prevention, remediation. *Action in Teacher Education*, Fall 1980, *2* (4), 29-34.

Kotsakis, J. Analysis of survey commentary still needed. *Chicago Union Teacher*, March 1978, p. 4.

Kyriacou, C. Coping actions and occupational stress among school teachers. *Research in Education*, 1981, (24), pp. 57-61.

Kyriacou, C. Stress, health, and schoolteachers: A comparison with other professions. *Cambridge Journal of Education*, 1980, 10, 154-159.

Kyriacou, C., & Sutcliffe, J. A model of teacher stress. *Educational Studies*, March 1978, 4, 1-6.

Lazarus, R. S. *Psychological stress and the coping process*. New York: McGraw Hill, 1966.

Lehmann, I. J., & Mehrens, W. A. *Educational research: Readings in focus*. New York: Holt Rinehart and Winston, Inc., 1971.

Leffingwell, R. J. The role of the middle school counselor in the reduction of stress in teachers. *Elementary School Guidance and Counseling*, April 1979, pp. 286-291.

Levi, L. Occupational stress - a psychophysiological view. *Occupational Mental Health*, 1973, 3, 6-9.

Levin, W. S. A word of caution. *Maryland State Teachers Association Action Line*, June 18, 1980 13, 2.

Levinson, H. Occupational stress - a psychoanalytical view. *Occupational Mental Health*, 1973, 3, 2-5.

Lortie, D. C. *Schoolteacher: A sociological study*. Chicago: The University of Chicago Press, 1975.

Margolis, B. L., Kroes, W. H., & Quinn, R. P. Job stress: An unlisted occupational hazard. Journal of Occupational Medicine, 1974, 10, 654-661.

Maslach, C. Job burnout - how people cope. Public Welfare, 36, 56-58.

Mattsson, K. D. Personality traits associated with effective teaching in rural and urban secondary schools. Journal of Educational Psychology, 1974, 66, 123-128.

McGuire, W. H. Teacher burnout. Today's Education, November-December 1979, p. 5.

Miles, R. H. Role requirements as sources of organizational stress. Journal of Applied Psychology, 1976, 61, 172-179.

Moe, D. Teacher burnout - a prescription. Today's Education, November-December 1979, pp. 35-36.

Moracco, J. C., Gray, P., & D'Arienzo, R. V. Stress in teaching: A comparison of perceived stress between special education and regular teachers. Paper presented at the Eastern Educational Research Association Annual Meeting, Philadephia, Pa., March 13, 1981.

Moracco, J., & McFadden, H. Counselor's role in reducing teacher stress. Unpublished research report, Auburn University, 1980.

Muse, J. Survival of stressed teachers. Washington, D.C.: National Education Association of the United States, 1980.

Muse, J. Teacher stress and ultimate burnout. Unpublished manuscript, November 1979. (Available from the National Education Association, Washington, D. C.)

Mygdal, W. K. The acquisition of stress management skills by student teachers: An outcome study of stress inoculation and anxiety management (Doctoral dissertation, Baylor University, 1978). Dissertation Abstracts International, 1978, 39, 2839A-2840A. (University Micro-films No. 7820669, 160)

National Association of Elementary School Principals. Good-bye Ms. Dove. The National Elementary Principal, June 1980, p. 6.

National Education Association, Department of Classroom Teachers. Fit to teach: A study of the health problems of teachers. Washington, D. C.: NEA, 1938.

National Education Association. Poll probes teacher dissatisfaction. NEA Reporter, September 1980, 19, 2.

National Education Association. Rankings of the states, 1979. Research Memo, Washington, D.C.: 1979.

National Education Association. Teachers' problems. Research Bulletin, 1967, 45, 116-117.

NEA survey investigates teacher attitudes, practices. Kappan, September 1980, 62, 49-52.

Needle, R. H., Griffin, T., & Svendsen, R. Occupational stress coping and health problems of teachers. The Journal of School Health, March 1981, 51, 175-181.

Needle, R. H., Griffin, T., Svendsen, R., & Berney, C. Teacher stress: Sources and consequences. The Journal of School Health, February 1980, pp. 96-99.

Newell, R. C. Teacher stress - warning: Teaching may be hazardous to your health. American Teacher, December 1978/January 1979, pp. 16-17.

Nie, N. H., Hull, C. H., Jenkins, J. G., Steinbrenner, K., & Bent, D. H. *Statistical Package for the Social Sciences, Second Edition.* New York: McGraw-Hill, 1975.

Olander, H. T., & Farrell, M. E. Professional problems of elementary teachers. *The Journal of Teacher Education,* Summer 1970, *21,* 276-280.

Parkay, F. W. Inner-city high school teachers: The relationship of personality traits and teaching style to environmental stress (Doctoral dissertation, The University of Chicago, 1978). *Dissertation Abstracts International,* 1978, *39,* 3479A-3480A.

Parsons, J. L. S. Anxiety and teaching competence (Doctoral dissertation, Stanford University, 1970). *Dissertation Abstracts International,* 1971, *31,* 4018. (University Microfilms No. 71-2867, 119)

Peck, L. A. A study of the adjustment difficulties of a group of women teachers. *Journal of Educational Psychology,* 1933, *27,* 401-416.

Pelletier, K. R. *Mind as healer, mind as slayer.* New York: Dell Publishing Company, 1977.

Pines, A., & Maslach, C. Characteristics of staff burnout in mental health settings. *Hospital & Community Psychiatry,* April 1978, *29,* 233-236.

Price, L. W. Organizational stress and job satisfaction of public high school teachers (Doctoral dissertation, Stanford University, 1970). *Dissertation Abstracts International,* 1971, *31,* 5727A-5728A. (University Microfilms No. 71-12976, 167)

Readers report on the tragedy of burnout. *Learning,* April 1979, pp. 76-77.

Reed, S. What you can do to prevent teacher burnout. *Elementary Principal,* 1979, *60,* 67-70.

Schwartz, E. N. Stresses in alternative school settings and how teachers cope with them: A psycho-social perspective (Doctoral dissertation, Harvard University, 1976). Dissertation Abstracts International, 1976, 37, 3540A-3541A. (University Microfilms No. 76-26753, 371)

Scrivens, R. The big click. Today's Education, November-December 1979, pp. 34-35.

Sellinger, S. An investigation of the effects of organizational climate and teacher anxiety on test anxiety of elementary school students (Doctoral dissertation, New York University, 1971). Dissertation Abstracts International, 1972, 32, 5515A-5516A. (University Micro-films No. 72-11494, 140)

Selye, H. (interviewed by L. Cherry) On the real benefits of eustress. Psychology Today, March 1978, pp. 60-64.

Selye, H. Stress without distress. New York: J. B. Lippincott Co., 1974.

Selye, H. The stress of life. New York: McGraw-Hill, 1956.

Selye, H. The stress of life, revised edition. New York: McGraw-Hill, 1976.

Sparks, D. C. A biased look at teacher job satisfaction. The Clearing House, May 1979, 52, 447-449.

Sparks, D. C. A teacher center tackles the issues. Today's Education, November-December 1979, pp. 37-39.

Statistical look at stress-survey reveals consistency. Chicago Union Teacher, March 1978, pp. 1; 3. (Article based on report prepared by D. Cichon of the RMC Research Corporation)

Stevenson, G. S., & Milt, H. Ten tips to reduce tension. *Today's Education*, March-April 1975, pp. 52-54.

Styles, K., & Cavanagh, G. Stress in teaching and how to handle it. *English Journal*, January 1977, 66, 76-79.

Survey analysis identifies management pressures as major issue. *Chicago Union Teacher*, March 1978, pp. 2-3. (Article based on report presented to American Educational Research Association by R. Koff)

Swick, K. J., & Hanley, P. E. *Stress and the classroom teacher*. Washington, D.C.: National Education Association, 1980.

Sylwester, R. Stress. *Instructor*, March 1977, 86, 72-76.

Tacoma's stress insurance plan. *Kappan*, 1979, 61, 254.

Take this test and try these tips on how to handle stress. *The Executive Educator*, April 1980, pp. 20-21.

Teacher burnout - how to cope when your world goes black. *Instructor*, January 1979, pp. 56-62.

Valencia, S. M. Anxiety cued verbal responses in student teachers (Doctoral dissertation, University of California, Los Angeles, 1970). *Dissertation Abstracts International*, 1971, 32, 3358A. University Microfilms No. 71-719, 96)

Walker, C. E. *Learn to relax, 13 ways to reduce tension*. Englewood Cliffs, New Jersey: Prentice-Hall, Inc., 1975.

Walley, W. Aspects of teacher health measured by survey. *Chicago Union Teacher*, March 1978, p. 4.

Walsh, D.   Classroom stress and teacher burnout. Kappan, 1979, 61, 253.

Weiskopf, P. E.   Burnout among teachers of exceptional children.   Exceptional Children, September 1980, 47, 18-23.

Wey, H. W.   Difficulties of beginning teachers. School Review, 1951, 51, 32-57.

Wield, B. S., & Hanes, C. A.   A dynamic conceptual framework of generalized adaptation to stressful stimuli.   Psychological Reports, 1976, 38, 319.

Yuenger, J.   Teacher burnout - our classroom crisis.   Chicago Tribune, February 1, 1981, pp. 1; 10.

APPENDIX A

CLARK'S (1980) TOSFQ

TEACHER OCCUPATIONAL STRESS FACTOR QUESTIONNAIRE

All of us occasionally feel bothered or stressed by certain kinds of things in our work. You are being asked to participate in a study deigned to identify the major occupational stress factors of class-room teachers. Your cooperation and honest responses in completing the surveys are earnestly requested. The responses you make will be treated confidentially; only the researcher will see your response. Your cooperation is appreciated.

(1) Indicate the extent to which each of the items on the following pages is stressful to <u>you</u> in your job by circling the appropriate number:

    (0) -not stressful
    (1) -somewhat stressful
    (2) -considerably stressful
    (3) -decidedly stressful
    (4) -extremely stressful

For example, if you feel the item is <u>considerably stressful</u> to you, then you would circle the number 2 for that item.

Example item: Having afternoon bus duty
0 1 2 3 4

(2) Mark your first impression and don't spend a lot of time on any one item.

(3) Please respond to every item.

                Thank you for your cooperation.

0 -not stressful
1 -somewhat stressful
2 -considerably stressful
3 -decidedly stressful
4 -extremely stressful

1. Trying to motivate students who do not want to learn 0 1 2 3 4

2. Feeling my salary is not equal to my duties and responsibilities 0 1 2 3 4

3. Feeling there is a lack of administrative support for teachers in my school 0 1 2 3 4

4. Working in a school where there is an atmosphere of conflict among teachers 0 1 2 3 4

5. Having students in my class/classes who talk constantly 0 1 2 3 4

6. Having to do school work at home to meet what is expected of me 0 1 2 3 4

7. Feeling my principal lacks insight into classroom problems 0 1 2 3 4

8. Feeling some teachers in my school are incompetent 0 1 2 3 4

9. Feeling too many parents are indifferent about school problems 0 1 2 3 4

10. Feeling my opinions are not valued by my principal 0 1 2 3 4

11. Feeling there is competition among teachers in my school rather than a team spirit of cooperation 0 1 2 3 4

12. Having to tell my students the same things over and over 0 1 2 3 4

0 -not stressful
1 -somewhat stressful
2 -considerably stressful
3 -decidedly stressful
4 -extremely stressful

13. Having insufficient opportunity for rest and preparation during the school day   0 1 2 3 4

14. Working for an inadequate salary   0 1 2 3 4

15. Feeling my principal gives me too little authority to carry out the responsibilities assigned to me   0 1 2 3 4

16. Planning and organizing learning activities for wide ability ranges   0 1 2 3 4

17. Feeling there is a lack of recognition for good teaching in my school   0 1 2 3 4

18. Feeling poor teacher/teacher relationships exist in my school   0 1 2 3 4

19. Feeling that a few difficult to discipline students take too much of my time away from other students   0 1 2 3 4

20. Feeling I cannot tell my principal in an open way how I feel about school related matters   0 1 2 3 4

21. Feeling my students do not adequately respond to my teaching   0 1 2 3 4

22. Having too little clerical help   0 1 2 3 4

23. Having a few teachers who do not carry their share of the load   0 1 2 3 4

24. Feeling I do not have adequate control of my students   0 1 2 3 4

0 - not stressful
1 - somewhat stressful
2 - considerably stressful
3 - decidedly stressful
4 - extremely stressful

25. Feeling there is a lack of parental involvement in solving school discipline problems   0 1 2 3 4

26. Feeling my principal is too aloof and detached from the classroom   0 1 2 3 4

27. Feeling that cliques exist among teachers in my school   0 1 2 3 4

28. Feeling my job does not provide the financial security I need   0 1 2 3 4

29. Feeling I never catch up with my work   0 1 2 3 4

30. Feeling that poor communications exist among teachers in my school   0 1 2 3 4

Demographic Information

    Fill in the demographic Information as requested.

Age: _____

Sex: _____ Female _____ Male

Marital Status: _____ Single
                        _____ Married
                        _____ Divorced
                        _____ Widowed

Sex of your principal: _____ Female _____ Male

What is the approximate enrollment of the school where you teach? _____

Number of years teaching experience: _____

Highest degree earned: _____ B.S. or B.A.
                              _____ M.S. or M.Ed.
                              _____ Ed.S
                              _____ Ed.D. or Ph.D.

What grade do you teach? _____ If you work in a departmentalized school, what subject/subjects do you teach? _____
_____
_____

Are you happy with your profession? _____

If you had your life to live over, would you become a teacher? _____

APPENDIX B

MODIFIED TOSFQ

MODIFIED TEACHER OCCUPATIONAL STRESS FACTOR QUESTIONNAIRE

You are being requested to participate in a study concerned with the occupational stress factors affecting classroom teachers. Your cooperation and sincerity are earnestly requested. Your responses will be treated confidentially. Please do not identify yourself on the answer sheet.

Please make all responses on the answer sheet provided. Make no marks on the survey instrument. All responses should be made with a number 2 lead pencil only. <u>Please</u> respond to every item.

Items 1-30 are concerned with identified factors of job-induced stress for teachers. Indicate the extent to which each of these items is stressful to you by marking carefully the corresponding response position on your answer sheet: (A) not stressful; (B) somewhat stressful; (C) considerably stressful; (D) decidedly stressful; (E) extremely stressful.

For example, if you feel the item is <u>considerably stressful</u> to you, then you would <u>fill in</u> position C for that item.

1. Trying to motivate students who do not want to learn

2. Feeling my salary is not equal to my duties and responsibilities

3. Feeling there is a lack of administrative support for teachers in my school

4. Working in a school where there is an atmosphere of conflict among teachers

5. Having students in my class/classes who talk constantly

6. Having to do school work at home to meet what is expected of me

7. Feeling my principal lacks insight into classroom problems

8. Feeling some teachers in my school are incompetent

9. Feeling too many parents are indifferent about school problems

10. Feeling my opinions are not valued by my principal

11. Feeling there is competition among teachers in my school rather than a team spirit of cooperation

12. Having to tell my students the same things over and over

13. Having insufficient opportunity for rest and preparation during the school day

14. Working for an inadequate salary

15. Feeling my principal gives me too little authority to carry out the responsibilities assigned to me

16. Planning and organizing learning activities for wide ability ranges

17. Feeling there is a lack of recognition for good teaching in my school

18. Feeling poor teacher/teacher relationships exist in my school

19. Feeling that a few difficult students take too much of my time away from other students

20. Feeling I cannot tell my principal in an open way how I feel about school related matters

21. Feeling my students do not adequately respond to my teaching

22. Having too little clerical help

23. Having a few teachers who do not carry their share of the load

24. Feeling I do not have adequate control of my students

25. Feeling there is a lack of parental involvement in solving school discipline problems

26. Feeling my principal is too aloof and detached from the classroom

27. Feeling that cliques exist among teachers in my school

28. Feeling my job does not provide the financial security I need

29. Feeling I never catch up with my work

30. Feeling that poor communications exist among teachers in my school

Items 31-50 are concerned with teachers' feelings about themselves and their students. Please indicate on your answer sheet how you feel about each by marking: (A) strongly agree; (B) agree; (C) neutral; (D) disagree; (E) strongly disagree.

31. Teachers have no bias or prejudices: All students look alike to a good teacher

32. Teachers should be calm; they should never display strong emotions

33. Teachers should not be responsible for their students' happiness

34. Teachers must be consistent at all times

35. Teachers should show the same degree of acceptance for all students

36. Teachers should not put their students' needs ahead of their own

37. Teachers are not responsible for their students' behavior

38. Teachers should not allow students to become aware of their (teachers') foibles or "hang ups"

39. Teachers should support each other by presenting a united front to students regardless of teachers' personal feelings, values, or convictions.

40. Teachers must protect students from failure and disappointments

41. If I don't set high standards for myself, I am likely to end up a second-rate person

42. People will probably think less of me if I made a mistake

43. If I canno t do something really well, there is little point in doing it at all

44. I should be upset if I make a mistake

45. It I try hard enough, I should be able to excel at anything I attempt

46. It is shameful for me to display weakness or foolish behavior

47. I shouldn't have to repeat the same mistakes many times

48. An average performance is bound to be unsatisfying to me

49. Failing at something important means I'm less of a person

50. If I scold myself for failing to live up to my expectations, it will help me do better in the future

Items 51-72 are concerned with commons symptoms of stress. What stress symptoms have you experienced on the job? Please respond to the frequency you have experienced the following symptoms. Mark carefully the corresponding response on your answer sheet: (A) never; (B) rarely; (C) sometimes; (D) often; (E) always.

51. Headaches
52. Stomach aches or tension
53. Back aches
54. Stiffness in the neck & shoulders
55. Elevated blood pressure
56. Fatigue
57. Crying
58. Forgetfulness
59. Yelling
60. Blaming
61. Bossiness
62. Compulsive eating
63. Worrying
64. Depression
65. Agitation
66. Impatience
67. Anger
68. Frustration
69. Loneliness
70. Powerlessness
71. Inflexibility
72. Compulsive smoking

Items 73-84 are concerned with common measures employed to relax. How often do you use these measures to relax? Mark carefully the corre-sponding response on your answer sheet: (A) never; (B) rarely; (C) some-times; (D) often; (E) always.

73. Take aspirin
74. Use tranquilizers or other medication
75. Drink coffee, coke, or eat frequently
76. Use relaxation techniques (meditation, yoga)
77. Use informal relaxation techniques (i.e., take time out for deep breathing, imagining pleasant scenes)
78. Exercise
79. Talk to someone you know
80. Leave your work area and go somewhere (time out, sick days, lunch away from your school, etc.)
81. Smoke
82. Use Humor
83. Have a drink after work to relax
84. Other

Items 85-99 are demographic data concerns. Please mark all answers on your answer sheet.

85. Age: (A) 21-30; (B) 31-40; (C) 41-50; (D) 51-60; (E) 60 or older

86. Sex: (A) Male; (B) Female

87. Marital Status: (A) Single; (B) Married; (C) Divorced; (D) Widowed

88. Race: (A) Caucasian; (B) Black; (C) Spanish Surname; (D) Asian; (E) Other

89. Highest Degree earned: (A) B.S. or B.A.; (B) M.S. or M.Ed.; (C) Ed.S.; (D) Ed.D. or Ph.D.

90. Number of years teaching experience: (A) 1-5; (B) 6-10; (C) 11-15; (D) 16-20; (E) 21 or more

91. Are you a special education teacher?: (A) Yes; (B) No

92. Type of school: (A) Elementary (K-6); (B) Middle (7-8) or Junior High (7-9); (C) High School (9-12); (D) Senior High School (10-12); (E) Special Education Center

93. School setting: (A) Rural; (B) Suburban; (C) Urban

94. School enrollment: (A) less than 200; (B) 200-400; (C) 400-600; (D) 600-800; (E) More than 800

95. Sex of your principal: (A) Male; (B) Female

96. How many days of school have you missed during the past year? (A) 0; (B) 1-3; (C) 4-7; (D) 8-11; (E) 12 or more

97. In your opinion, was stress you experienced in teaching a factor in the number of days you missed? (A) Yes; (B) No

98. If you answered "Yes" for 97, what percent of days taken were because of stress?: (A) 10%; (B) 20%; (C) 50%; (D) 70%; (E) 90%

99. If you had your life to live over, would you become a teacher?: (A) Yes; (B) No

APPENDIX C

Table 24

Items 1-30 and Their Factor Locations on TOSFQ and Modified TOSFQ

Item		TOSFQ	Modified TOSFQ
1.	Trying to motivate students who do not want to learn	1	2
2.	Feeling my salary is not equal to my duties and responsibilities	1	3
3.	Feeling there is a lack of administrative support for teachers in my school	2	1
4.	Working in a school where there is an atmosphere of conflict among teachers	3	4
5.	Having students in my class/classes who talk constantly	4	2
6.	Having to do school work at home to meet what is expected of me	5	5
7.	Feeling my principal lacks insight into classroom problems	2	1
8.	Feeling some teachers in my school are incompetent	3	4
9.	Feeling too many parents are indifferent about school problems	1	2

Table 24 (Continued)

Items 1-30 and Their Factor Locations
on TOSFQ and Modified TOSFQ

Item		TOSFQ	Modified TOSFQ
10.	Feeling my opinions are not valued by my principal	2	1
11.	Feeling there is competition among teachers in my school rather than a team spirit of cooperation	3	4
12.	Having to tell my students the same things over and over	4	2
13.	Having insufficient opportunity for rest and preparation during the school day	5	5
14.	Working for an inadequate salary	1	3
15.	Feeling my principal gives me too little authority to carry out the responsibilities assigned to me	2	1
16.	Planning and organizing learning activities for wide ability ranges	4	5
17.	Feeling there is a lack of recognition for good teaching in my school	2	1
18.	Feeling poor teacher/teacher relationships exist in my school	3	4

Table 24 (Continued)

Items 1-30 and Their Factor Locations
on TOSFQ and Modified TOSFQ

Item		TOSFQ	Modified TOSFQ
19.	Feeling that a few difficult students take too much of my time away from other students	1	2
20.	Feeling I cannot tell my principal in an open way how I feel about school related matters	2	1
21.	Feeling my students do not adequately respond to my teaching	4	2
22.	Having too little clerical help	5	5
23.	Having a few teachers who do not carry their share of the load	3	4
24.	Feeling I do not have adequate control of my students	4	2
25.	Feeling there is a lack of parental involvement in solving school discipline problems	1	2
26.	Feeling my principal is too aloof and detached from the classroom	2	1

Table 24 (Continued)

Items 1-30 and Their Factor Locations
on TOSFQ and Modified TOSFQ

Item		TOSFQ	Modified TOSFQ
27.	Feeling that cliques exist among teachers in my school	3	4
28.	Feeling my job does not provide the financial security I need	1	3
29.	Feeling I never catch up with my work	5	5
30.	Feeling that poor communications exist among teachers in my school	3	4

INDEX

Absence of insight, 94
Absenteeism, 3, 4, 28, 32, 62-64
Action constraint, 18
Actual stressors, 13-14
Addiction to Alcohol, 3, 28, 32-33
Administrative Support, 25, 65, 70-71, 76-79, 84, 87, 91, 92, 94-94, 98
Alabama, 55, 94, 97-98
Alley, R., 12, 19, 20, 22, 25, 26, 27, 29, 32, 34, 35
Alschuler, A.S., 19
American Association of School Administration, 1
Analysis of variance, 77
Anderson, B., 16, 19, 20, 25, 33, 34, 35
Anxiety, 1, 3, 16, 26-27
Appraisal Mechanism, 13-14
Ary, D., 60
Auburn University General Purpose Scan Forms, 60

Ban, J. R., 2, 12, 14, 19, 20, 22, 25, 26, 27, 28, 32
Bardo, P., 1, 5, 22, 26, 27, 28
Bartley, S. H., 26
Bates, H., 20
Baugh, D. S., 42
Behavioral effects of stress, 32-33
Behavioral stress symptoms, 25-26, 28, 32
Beane, W. E., 20
Bensky, J. M., 20, 38
Benson, H., 34, 36
Bent, D. H., 64
Bentz, W. K., 6, 39
Berger, M., 3, 22, 25, 26, 27, 29, 30, 31, 32
Biographical information, 41
Biofeedback techniques, 36
Block, A. M., 3, 19, 24, 25, 26, 27, 29, 30, 31, 32, 34, 35, 40
Broder, F., 11, 20, 22, 25, 26, 33, 34, 35
Brown, B. B., 36
Brown, L., 19, 22, 33, 34
Bry, A., 34
Burchfield, S.R., 3, 11, 13
Burnout, 11-12, 14-16, 26-33, 37-39
Burns, D. D., 6, 57, 101

Calhoun, G. L., 34, 35, 36
Cardinell, C. F., 22, 26, 27, 28, 29, 33
Causes of stress, 13-26
Cavanagh, G., 22
Central Administrative Area, 58
Cherry, L., 26
Chicago Teachers Union, 1, 40-41
Cichon, D. J., 17-18, 24-25, 30, 34, 40-41, 92-95, 98
Clark, E. H., 5, 7, 39, 42-44, 55-65, 92-99
Classroom control, 20
Classroom crime, 19-20
Clusters of stressors, 17-19
Coates, T. J., 1, 5, 20, 22
Cochrane, R., 17, 33-36
Collegial Relationships, 43, 56, 65, 69, 96
Collins, D., 16, 24-26, 33-35, 98
Comparison of Stress Factors, 92-98
Cooper, C.L., 22, 25, 26
Coping mechanisms, 5, 14-15, 33-37, 58
Counselors, 4, 38
Cox, 13
Cronbach's coefficient alpha, 43-44
Curriculum specialist, 38

Dale, R. L., 26, 29, 30, 41
D'Alonzo, B. J., 38, 39
Death due to stress, 32
Definition of stress, 7, 11-12
Demographic variables, 4, 5, 45, 46-55, 61
Dependent variable, 76
Depression, 3, 27
Descriptive research, 60, 61
Disability
  emotional, 2
  physical, 2
Discipline, 20
Distress, 1, 17
Dixon, B., 20, 26, 35, 38
Doing-a-good-job concern, 17, 18
Drug addiction, 33

Edgerton, J. W., 6, 39
Education, 5, 6
Educational research, 6
Eigenvalues, 43, 97
Elementary Schools, 3, 9, 46, 49, 59
Elementary teacher, 6
Emotional disability, 2
Emotional exhustion, 18, 15, 16, 29, 32
Endocrine system, 32
Enrollment, student, 48
Environmental stressors, 19, 24-26, 98
Eustress, 1, 17
Exceptional children, 37

"F" test, 77, 78
Factor Analysis Procedures, 61, 64, 65, 67, 94, 95
Farrell, M. E., 25
Fatigue, 14
Federal government, 47
Federal Legislation, 20, 24
Federal regulation, 4
Female teachers, 1
Financial Security, 73, 77, 86, 87, 91, 96, 99, 103, 104, 67, 72, 81, 88, 92, 95, 99
Flanders Interaction Analysis, 42
Freudenberger, H. J., 27-29, 34, 35

Genitourinary/digestive system, 31
Georgia, 55, 94, 97
Goodall, R., 19, 25, 33, 34
Gouse, A. S., 20
Griffin, T., 36
Group Instruction, 43, 56, 69
Guilt, 34

Hanes, C. A., 13
Hanley, P. E., 21-24
Harlin, V. K., 4, 26-35
Harrison, 22, 27
Health Opinion Survey, 39
Hendricks, C. G., 23
Hendrickson, B., 26-35
Hicks, F. P., 1
High blood pressure, 29

High School, 46, 49, 59, 81, 100
Hinkle, L. E., 13
Hollister, S. G., 6, 39
Home Environmental Stressor, 13, 16, 17
Homeostasis, 6, 7, 11, 12, 44
Hospitalization, 3
Hull, C. H., 64
Humphrey, J. H., 34
HUmphrey, J. N., 34
Hunter, M., 1
Hyptertension, 26

Immunological system, 30
Independent variable, 76, 79
Individual Characteristics, 14, 24
IPAT Anxiety Scale, 42
Instruments used in Stress Studies, 39-41, 55
Internal consistency, 43, 44, 56
Interpersonal transfers, 24
Involuntary transfers, 24

Jacobs, L. C., 60
Jenkins, J. G., 64
Jerrick, S. J., 4
Job Overload, 43, 56, 64, 70, 93, 96
Job satisfaction, 23
Junior High School, 23, 46, 49, 59, 81, 100

Kahn, R. L., 21, 23, 29, 31, 32
Kaisers Varimax, 43
Kerlinger, F. N., 76
Koff, R. H., 18, 24, 25, 34, 40, 41, 92-95
Kossack, S. W., 34, 35
Kotsakis, J., 22, 25
Kroes, W. H., 29
Kyriacou, C., 3, 11, 13, 33, 35

Learning Centers, 34
Leffingwell, R. J., 22, 26-28, 33-35
Levi, L., 12
Lifes changes, 16
Life Events Inventory, 17
Limitations, 8, 9
Listwise Deletion, 77
Low job productivity, 3

Mainstreaming, 20, 26
Management tension concerns, 18
Manifest Anxiety Scale, 42
Margolis, B. L., 29, 31
Marital Status, 4, 49, 61, 62, 74
Marshall, J., 22, 25-28
Maslach, C., 16, 27, 28, 35
McFadden, H., 8, 13, 14, 29, 30-34 7, 11, 12, 27-29
McGuire, W. H., 18, 21, 22, 26-28, 16, 19, 20, 24-26
Measuring perceived stress, 73
Mental exhaustion, 16
Mental health, 1, 4
Metropolitan, 47
Middle High School, 49, 59
Miles, R. H., 22
Milt, H., 19, 22-25
(MMPI) -The Minnesota Multiphasic Personality Inventory, 40
Minnesota Teacher Attitude Inventory, 42
Model of Stress, 13, 15, 16, 24, 44, 45
Moe, D., 33-35
Monogram, G. E., 29, 32
Moracco, J. C., 8, 13, 14, 29-34, 7, 11, 12, 26-29
Multiple regression analysis, iv, 61, 74-76, 78-80
Muse, J., 2, 3, 29-32

National Association of Elementary School Principals, 32
National Education Association, 1, 2, 25, 48, 102
Needle, R. H., 36
Nervous
  breakdowns, 1
  symptoms, 1
Nervous system, 31
Newell, R. C., 3, 22, 25, 29-32
Nie, N. H., 76

Oblique rotation, 71-73, 75, 65, 66, 70
Obsesive-Compulsive Ideation, 4, 6, 21, 61, 62, 74, 83, 84, 88, 90, 101
Occupational stressor, 5-8, 13, 16, 42, 61, 90

Parents, 20, 67
Pedagogical functions concerns, 17-19
Pedhazur, E. J., 76
Pelletier, K. R., 34, 36
Perceived Occupational Stress Scale, 41
Perceived Teacher Stress, iv, 74, 76, 79
Perception mediation, 44
Personal achievements, 48
Personal Stress, 22
Physical disability, 2
Physical exercise, 34
Physical stress symptoms, 26-32
Post hoc analyses, 76, 79
Potential stressors, 13
Predictor variables, 74, 76, 77
Premature death, 4, 32
Principal, 6, 8, 23, 59, 60, 74, 94
  male, 9, 61, 66, 68, 82, 83, 88, 104, 8, 54, 61,
  62, 77, 83, 100
  female, 9, 61, 66, 68, 82, 83, 88, 104, 8, 54,
  61, 62, 77, 83, 100
Principal-Teacher-Relationships, 43, 56
Priority Concerns, 17, 95
Professional burnout, 5, 6, 14
Professional Inadequacy, 43, 56, 65, 67, 68
Professional stress, 22, 23
Prolonged manifestations, 14
Psychic demands, 12
Psychological homeostasis, 44
Psychological Stress Symptoms, 26-28, 32

Quinn, R. P., 29, 31, 32
Razavieh, A., 60
Regression Analyses, 74
Relationships with Teachers, 65, 72, 83, 85, 92,
  97-99, 96, 102, 104
Relaxation techniques, 34
Representative Assembly, 2
Research, 1, 3, 39-44, 46, 47, 58-60, 102-104,
  107-109
Resolution E., 2
Resiratory system, 30
Robertson, A., 19, 36-39, 17, 33-36
Rokeach Dogmatism Scale, 42
Role ambiguity, 22

Role conflict, 22
Roles of resource teacher, 38, 39
Rural, 47

Scheffe test, 77
Schizophrenia, 32
School Administrator, 4, 34
School Administrator Stress Survey, 25, 26, 42
School settings, 4, 54, 61, 62, 74, 79, 83, 87-88, 92, 94
  rural, 47, 48, 54, 77, 81, 83, 88, 90, 94, 98, 102
  urban, 47, 48, 54, 77, 81, 83, 88, 90, 94, 98, 102
Scrivens, R., 31
Secondary Teacher, 6
Self-expectations, 22
Selye, H., 1, 3, 6, 11, 17, 27
Senior High School, 46, 59, 81, 100
Sex of Principal, 4, 54, 61, 62, 77, 83, 87, 88, 92, 100
Shaw, S. F., 20, 38
Skeletal-muscular system, 30
Social Readjustment Rating Scale, 40
Societal Stressor, 13, 17
Somantic demands, 12
Sparks, D. C., 21, 22, 25
Special Education, 4, 7, 37, 48, 49, 53, 61, 62, 74, 79, 87, 100
Special Education Centers, 48, 49, 53
State Regulation, 4
State-Trait Anxiety Inventory, 42
Stevenson, G.S., 19, 22, 24
Stress
  burnout, 26, 28, 29, 32
  causes of, 16, 17
  cluster of stressors, 17
  coping mechanisms, 14, 33-36
  definition of, 3, 7, 11, 12, 44, 45
  environmental, 19, 24, 25, 98
  factor, 7
  generated by, 22
  intensity of, 2
  intrapersonal, 19, 22, 23
  job related, 18

    management, 2
    models, 13-16
    occupational, 5, 10, 11
    personal, 22
    physiological, 3, 26
    pleasant, 1
    process, 13, 29-32, 103
    professional, 22-23
    psychic, 3
    research, 1, 3, 39-44, 46, 47, 58-60
    Special Ed Teachers, 4, 37-39, 45
    Study Instruments, 39-42
    Symptoms, 26-28
    Teacher, 1-4, 20-23, 44, 62, 63, 74, 76
    Theory, 3
    Unpleasant, 1, 16
Stressful Situation Scale, 41
Student discipline, 18, 19, 93, 103
Sutcliff, J., 3, 11, 13
Svendsen, R., 36
Swick, K. J., 21, 23, 24
Sylwester, R., 16, 20, 26

Tacoma's stress, 2, 25
Task Overload, 65, 70, 84-88, 92, 93, 96, 100
Teacher, 7, 20, 21, 49, 53-55
    absenteeism, 3, 28, 62-64
    anxiety, 1, 16, 26, 42, 103
    Belief System, 4, 7, 21, 56, 61, 62, 74, 90, 92
    burnout, 2, 5, 14, 16, 27, 37, 38
    Elementary, 6
    expected roles of, 21, 22
    feelings, 56, 76, 94, 95
    mental health, 1
    organizations, 2
    retirement, 2
    salary, 98
    Secondary, 6
    self-actualization, 104
    self-esteem, 12-14, 44, 46
    single, 49, 62, 74, 90
    Special Education, 4, 7, 37-39, 79
    stress, 1, 2, 11, 23-39, 62, 76
    well being, 12-14
    widowed, 49, 90

Teacher Occupational Stress Factor Questionnaire -(TOSFQ), iv, 5, 42, 43, 46, 55, 61, 62, 65, 65-67, 70, 73-79, 81, 83, 84, 89, 91, 92, 93, 101
Teacher-Principal Professional Relationships, 65, 68
Teaching Stress Events Inventory -(TSEI), 40
Team teaching, 34
Tension, 3, 16, 24
Test Anxiety Questionnaire, 42
Thoreson, C.E., 5, 20, 22, 23, 25
Time management skills, 35
Type of school, 4, 59, 60, 74, 79, 81, 87, 88, 92, 100

Urban, 47, 54

Vandalism, 19, 20
Varimax factor's, 70
Veteran teachers, 5, 99
Violence, 17-20, 40, 93, 94

Walker, C. E., 34
Walley, W., 29-32
Walsh, D., 1, 3, 5, 6, 31, 32
Washington, D. C., 9, 46, 58
Weiskopf, P. E., 21, 26, 27-28, 34-36, 37
Wey, H. W., 20, 27
Wield, B. S., 13
Wiseman, D. E., 38, 39
Woods, S. L., 34-36
Working with students, 67, 71, 79-81, 87, 92, 94, 98, 100, 105

Years teaching experience, 4, 59, 60, 74, 77, 83, 87, 92
Yuenger, J., 20, 24-26